Daniel B Lancaster

LIVING WATERS

*A 30-Day Journey Through
the Lord's Prayer*

For Elaine—Your name means "bright and shining light" and you are one to all those around you. So grateful that late in life I found love again

Living Waters: Discovering God's Abundance—A 30-Day
Journey Through the Lord's Prayer
© Daniel B. Lancaster, 2024
Published by:
Lightkeeper Books
http://www.lightkeeperbooks.com/
ISBN: 9798303183575 (Hardcover)
ISBN: 9798303180932 (Paperback)
Printed in the United States.

TABLE OF CONTENTS

PREFACE

This book comes with a special gift: *A Journey of Blessings: 40 Days with God in Prayer*. This faith-building toolkit includes:

- 40 Prayers for Your Heart - Simple, heartfelt prayers to bring strength and peace to your day. Use them for your quiet moments with God and enjoy the included audio version to listen wherever you are.

- 40 Quotes to Lift Your Spirit - Inspiring and hope-filled quotes to brighten your journey. They're like small flashlights of courage for your heart.

- 40 Scriptures to Grow By - Bible verses that plant seeds of faith, offering God's promises to guide and grow you spiritually.

You can download this gift to face life's challenges with confidence and grow deeper in faith. Go to:

https://lightkeeperbooks.com/gift

Every blessing,
Daniel B. Lancaster

PROLOGUE

Prayer has a way of meeting us in our moments of greatest need, becoming a lifeline that draws us closer to God. When my family and I left the mission field in Myanmar and relocated to Thailand, I felt an ache for the people and the work we had left behind. Years of ministry had connected us deeply to those communities, and stepping away felt like severing a part of my heart. Despite the physical distance, I found solace in prayer—particularly in the Lord's Prayer. Those familiar words became more than a ritual; they became my anchor to God and my connection to Myanmar. As I prayed, "Your kingdom come," I trusted that God's work would continue, even if I could no longer see it firsthand.

Over the next year, those prayers bore fruit in ways I could not have imagined. What began as a small group of 30 house churches multiplied to over 600. Friends shared testimonies of transformed lives, healed relationships, and entire communities coming to faith. The Lord's Prayer had become a river of living water, flowing far beyond my reach and refreshing the hearts of those I had carried in prayer.

This is the power of prayer. It bridges gaps we cannot cross, touches people's lives we may never meet, and aligns us with God's purposes. As you embark on this devotional journey, my hope is that you, too, will experience the living waters of prayer that refresh, restore, and reach beyond what you can see.

God's Blueprint for Devotion

The Shema is one of the most foundational prayers in Scripture, recited daily by God's people as a declaration of love and devotion. It calls us to love the Lord with all our heart, soul, mind, and strength, shaping every aspect of our being. This prayer is more than words; it is a call to action—a way to center our lives on God's love and let it flow outward into everything we do.

- *Heart* represents our emotions and desires. Loving God with our heart means letting His love shape what we long for and cherish.

- *Soul* signifies our identity and purpose. Loving God with our soul means aligning who we are with His will.

- *Mind* reflects our thoughts and beliefs. Loving God with our mind means letting His truth guide how we think and perceive the world.

- *Strength* points to our actions and resources. Loving God with our strength means living out our faith through service and stewardship.

When we live out the Shema, our love for God transforms our lives and overflows into our relationships, our communities, and even the systems that shape our world.

A Path to Transformation

The Lord's Prayer is not just a personal conversation with God; it is a roadmap for bringing His kingdom to earth. Each line invites us to align with God's will, allowing His love to flow through us into the spheres of influence that define our lives. When prayed with the Shema in mind, the

Lord's Prayer becomes a powerful guide to loving God fully and loving others deeply.

- *Heart:* "Our Father in heaven..." reminds us of God's loving presence. Pray for those you care about, asking God to fill their hearts with peace and joy.

- *Soul:* "Your kingdom come..." calls us to seek God's purpose in the lives of those who feel lost or disconnected. Pray for their transformation and spiritual growth.

- *Mind:* "Give us this day our daily bread" directs us to seek clarity and wisdom for ourselves and others facing difficult decisions.

- *Strength:* "Lead us not into temptation but deliver us from evil" encourages us to pray for resilience and courage, both for ourselves and for those who feel overwhelmed by life's challenges.

As you pray these words, remember that each line is not just for personal growth but for the renewal of every sphere of influence in your life.

Six Spheres of Influence

Six interconnected spheres shape our lives—our Household, Neighborhood, Community, State, Nation, and World. Each sphere presents unique opportunities for God's work and distinct challenges that require intentional prayer.

- *Household:* Our closest relationships form the foundation of our lives. Pray for love, trust, and healing in your home.

- *Neighborhood:* Friendships and local connections bring joy but can face challenges like misunderstanding or isolation. Lift up your neighbors in prayer, asking for God's grace to sustain those bonds.

- *Community:* Faith communities and shared spaces offer opportunities for purpose and growth. Pray for unity, mission, and focus to reflect God's love to those in need.

- *State:* Larger systems often face challenges like prejudice and apathy. Pray for empathy and service to permeate workplaces and public spaces.

- *Nation:* Political division and moral compromise can disrupt unity. Pray for leaders and citizens to seek wisdom and justice that reflect God's kingdom.

- *World:* Global conflicts and neglect of creation require prayer for peace, compassion, and stewardship, embodying God's love for all people.

Praying for these spheres allows God's presence to flow through us, bringing restoration and peace to every area of our lives.

A Journey of Living Waters

Prayer is the thread that connects us to God's heart and aligns us with His purposes. As you walk through this devotional journey, consider how the Lord's Prayer and the Shema can guide you in transforming your heart, soul, mind, and strength. Each prayer becomes a ripple, spreading God's love into the six spheres of your life and beyond.

This journey is not just about personal growth but about becoming a vessel of God's love and justice. As you lift your voice in prayer, trust that God is working—through you and beyond you—bringing His kingdom to earth as it is in heaven.

NOTES:

USING THIS DEVOTIONAL

Each day's devotion offers a sacred rhythm—a journey to deepen your relationship with God and bring His presence into every part of your life. Picture yourself starting the day in stillness, soaking in Jesus' teachings, aligning your heart through prayer, and extending His love to those around you. This devotional provides a practical yet transformative framework, designed to renew your spirit and help you walk with purpose each day.

Beside Quiet Waters

Begin your devotional time in *Beside Quiet Waters*, where you pause and listen to God through His Word. Each day starts with Scripture and reflections that calm your heart and refocus your mind:

> *"Be still, and know that I am God"*
> *(Psalm 46:10)*

This sacred moment invites you to meet with God before the day's demands press in. Imagine yourself in a serene corner, the sunlight warming your face, as God's truth settles the noise of your thoughts. Let the Scriptures fill you with peace, offering clarity for the day ahead and anchoring you in His presence.

Even five minutes in this stillness can transform your perspective, reminding you of God's unfailing presence and preparing you to face the day with faith and hope.

Rivers of Living Water

Move from reflection to renewal in *Rivers of Living Water*, where Jesus' teachings flow into your daily life. This section illuminates how His words bring wisdom for your challenges and guidance for your decisions: _ "Whoever believes in me, as Scripture has said, rivers of living water will flow from within them." (John 7:38).

Jesus' teachings offer insight into relationships, work, and the choices you make each day. His words are not abstract—they are active, shaping the way you love, think, and act. Trust the Holy Spirit to help these truths take root, transforming not only your actions but also your heart.

Through Rivers of Living Water, you will experience the refreshment of God's wisdom and the courage to walk in faith, no matter what you face.

Deep Calls to Deep

Enter into deeper reflection in *Deep Calls to Deep*, where you meditate on God's Word and its impact on your heart. Let this time be a dialogue with God, as you explore areas where He is calling you to trust Him more fully: "Deep calls to deep in the roar of your waterfalls" (Psalm 42:7).

Use this prayer framework to guide your connection with Him:

Heart Prayers

Share your joys, burdens, and desires with God, trusting Him to fill your heart with peace and love.

Soul Prayers

Offer your longings and fears to God, asking Him to align your will with His perfect plan.

Mind Prayers

Seek God's wisdom to discern truth and navigate challenges with clarity.

Strength Prayers

Depend on God's power to sustain you, equipping you to live out His calling.

~

Let these prayers renew and align your spirit, equipping you to walk in God's strength throughout the day. This devotional rhythm invites you into God's presence and equips you to carry His truth into every part of your life. Step into this journey each day with expectation, knowing that He is with you, guiding you to reflect His love and light wherever you go.

DAY 1

Hallowed Be Your Name in Our Home

Our Father which art in heaven,
Hallowed be thy name.
(Matthew 6:9, KJV)

The morning light filters gently through the curtains, mirroring the renewing mercy of God. A family gathers, their voices lifting in unison: "Hallowed be thy name." These words are an invitation to sanctify the ordinary, turning moments like a shared breakfast or a simple prayer into acts of worship. The holiness of God transforms every corner of our lives when we open our hearts to Him. What might change in your home if every interaction carried the light of God's holiness?

BESIDE QUIET WATERS

Homes are sanctuaries not because of their design but through the grace they radiate. Imagine forgiveness at the dinner table softening hearts or a mother's whispered prayer transforming chaos into peace. The gentle laughter of children and the healing balm of an apology both reflect Psalm 96:8: 'Ascribe to the Lord the glory due his name.' What moments today can sanctify your home as a lighthouse of His love?

The Shema calls us to love God with all our heart, soul, mind, and strength—a love that overflows into our homes. A family's faith is like a garden, nurtured by shared prayer, words of encouragement, and acts of forgiveness. A child learning to pray through a parent's example or a guest welcomed with warmth testifies to God's love. By choosing patience, kindness, and joy, we create ripples of His presence that touch every life we encounter. How will you cultivate these seeds of faith today?

The world celebrates possessions and status, but God calls us to humility and service. A heartfelt apology can transform tension into peace, while an encouraging word can bring hope to a weary heart. When we prioritize love over appearance and faith over material pursuits, our homes become reflections of His kingdom. Pray. Forgive. Encourage. Let your actions glorify God and draw others to His presence.

RIVERS OF LIVING WATER

Prayer does not require eloquence, just an open heart. Picture a grandmother quietly praying for her family at the kitchen table or a child whispering their worries to God. These prayers, simple yet profound, transform ordinary homes into sanctuaries. Make prayer a central rhythm in your family life—inviting God's presence to flow freely. How can you carve out space for prayer that strengthens your home today?

The Holy Spirit gently guides us into prayer, removing pretense and leading us to God's heart. When we lift up our homes, strained relationships find healing, and peace replaces anxiety. Trust His prompting to bring life and hope into your family. Perhaps He'll nudge you to apologize to a loved one, speak encouragement, or intercede for a neighbor. How will you respond to His call today?

Establishing a daily rhythm of prayer strengthens the spiritual foundation of your home. Dedicate a cozy corner for prayer or encourage your family to join you at the dinner table for a moment of shared gratitude. Let the Spirit transform your home through consistent prayer, allowing His love to radiate into every conversation and action. How will you let prayer be the heartbeat of your home?

DEEP CALLS TO DEEP

Reflect on how the phrase "Hallowed be thy name" resonates within the walls of your home. Are there areas where God's presence needs to be more fully invited? Even the smallest act of faith—a prayer before a meal, a kind word spoken in love, or an intentional moment of gratitude—can hallow His name in transformative ways. Consider surrendering control over areas where worry has taken root, trusting God's power to bring peace. By weaving acts of faith into the fabric of your day, your home becomes a living testimony to God's holiness and grace.

Heart Prayer

Dear Heavenly Father,

Fill our home with Your peace. Transform brokenness into wholeness and worry into trust. Help us honor Your name in every interaction, creating a sanctuary of Your love.

Soul Prayer

Lord Jesus,

Reveal the purpose You have for each member of our household. Strengthen our faith and our relationships so that we may reflect Your love and values in every moment.

Mind Prayer

Holy Spirit,

Shape our thoughts with the power of Your truth, Lord, so that we may walk daily in wisdom and grace, honoring You in every step we take.

Strength Prayer

God Three-in-One,

Instill in us the resilience to remain faithful, even in the face of trials. May we rest in the assurance of Your steadfast presence, drawing strength from Your unchanging love.

For Thine is the kingdom, Lord Jesus
Thine is the power, Holy Spirit
And Thine is the glory, Heavenly Father,
forever. Amen.

~

A home shaped by God's love becomes a foundation for spiritual growth and renewal. Each act of kindness, word of encouragement, and moment of stillness creates space for His Spirit to work. Today, consider how your home can reflect His heart—whether through a shared prayer, a gesture of forgiveness, or a commitment to gratitude. Trust that He is nurturing your household into a place of peace and purpose.

NOTES:

DAY 2

Hallowed Be Your Name in Our Neighborhood

Our Father in heaven, hallowed be
your name.
(Matthew 6:9, NIV)

The neighborhood begins to stir as sunlight washes over front yards, mailboxes, and sidewalks. The words of the Lord's Prayer, "Our Father in heaven, hallowed be your name," remind us that God's presence is not confined to private spaces but extends into our neighborhoods. His holiness is reflected in the small details of life: a child's laughter, the morning greetings of neighbors, or the gentle sway of trees in the breeze. God's name is hallowed when we recognize His presence in our shared spaces and live in ways that reflect His love. How can you bring His holiness to life in your neighborhood today?

BESIDE QUIET WATERS

Mrs. Johnson, a widow with a heart full of care, spends her mornings tending her roses. Her flowers are beautiful, but it is her acts of kindness that bloom most brightly. When the Johnsons, a new family, move in next door, she shows up with cookies and a handwritten note, making them feel at home. Across the street, David's laughter fills the air as he plays soccer with friends. These simple moments—acts of kindness, bursts of joy—are reminders that God's love is tangible. Each interaction, however ordinary, becomes a way to hallow God's name and bring His grace to life.

God longs for our neighborhoods to reflect His kingdom, where peace, compassion, and connection thrive. The Shema's command to love God with all our heart, soul, mind, and strength flows outward into loving others. Picture a neighborhood where fences become places of connection rather than separation, and streets become pathways of kindness and forgiveness. God's love can transform simple streets into sanctuaries of grace. What would your neighborhood look like if every interaction reflected His love? Every act of encouragement or reconciliation sows seeds that honor His name and grow unity in the spaces we share.

The world often tells us to retreat inward, guarding our time and space. God invites us to break down those walls and engage outwardly. Let your words and actions hallow His name by reflecting His love. Speak encouragement to someone who feels unseen. Lend a hand to a struggling neighbor or offer a welcoming smile to someone new. By stepping outside your comfort zone, you create opportunities for God's presence to be felt. Imagine your neighborhood as a place where no one feels isolated, and everyone experiences the warmth of God's grace through the kindness of His people.

RIVERS OF LIVING WATER

Prayer shapes the heart of a neighborhood, weaving God's presence into every interaction. Jesus often sought solitude in prayer, finding quiet spaces to commune with His Father. He showed us that even in the busyness of life, prayer brings clarity and connection. Find your own moments of stillness to pray for your neighborhood. Your porch, a park bench, or a peaceful walk can become a sacred space to bring your neighbors' needs before God. Pray for unity where there is division, peace where there is turmoil, and comfort where there is pain. These prayers transform ordinary spaces into holy ground and align your heart with God's desires for your community.

The Holy Spirit moves within us, empowering us to see our neighborhoods as God does. He transforms mundane moments into opportunities for impact. Allow Him to guide your prayers and reveal needs you may not see at first glance. The Spirit may prompt you to check on a lonely neighbor, offer encouragement to someone in distress, or simply be present in a moment of connection. As you pray, trust that God's love is working through you to bring transformation to your neighborhood. The Spirit's whispers can lead to small acts that ripple into profound change.

Combine your prayers with action to reflect God's love in tangible ways. Host a neighborhood gathering to foster connections or offer to mow a lawn or bring groceries to someone who needs help. A simple act of kindness, done with God's love, can hallow His name in ways you may not realize. Your presence in someone's life can be a shining light of hope and a reflection of God's care. Let prayer fuel your actions, and let your actions bring life to your prayers, creating a cycle of love and transformation in your community.

DEEP CALLS TO DEEP

The phrase, "Hallowed be your name," invites us to bring God's holiness into the heart of our neighborhoods. What areas of your community need His presence most? Reflect on the opportunities to share His love and grace, even by the smallest gestures. Offering a smile, sharing a meal, or initiating a kind word can be a reflection of God's holiness. Ask God to reveal the needs of those around you and to use you to meet them. Trust that He can magnify even the simplest acts of faith, creating ripples of transformation that extend far beyond your vision.

Heart Prayer

> *Dear Heavenly Father,*
>
> *Pour out Your peace on our neighborhoods, mending divisions and restoring unity. May Your love fill every street and home, bringing healing and joy to all who live there.*

Soul Prayer

> *Lord Jesus,*

Awaken in our neighborhoods a longing for Your presence. Bring hope to the discouraged, strength to the weary, and joy to the brokenhearted. May our relationships reflect Your love.

Mind Prayer

Holy Spirit,

Grant us divine wisdom to perceive the needs of our neighbors clearly. Equip us with the courage to meet those needs through the boundless love and compassion of Christ.

Strength Prayer

God Three-in-One,

Prepare our hearts, Lord, to serve others with humility and boldness. May every word and action radiate Christ's love, inspiring hope and faith in those we encounter.

For Thine is the kingdom, Lord Jesus
Thine is the power, Holy Spirit
And Thine is the glory, Heavenly Father,
forever. Amen.

~

Your neighborhood is an extension of God's love, offering opportunities for meaningful connection. Each interaction—whether lending a helping hand, sharing a thoughtful word, or simply being present—reveals His grace. Today, pray for God to show you how to encourage someone nearby. Trust that even small steps will strengthen bonds and reflect His kingdom.

NOTES:

DAY 3

Hallowed Be Your Name in Our Community

Our Father in heaven, help us to
honor your name.
(Matthew 6:9, CEV)

A community thrives in its shared moments: laughter rising from local coffee shops, friendly exchanges at farmer's markets, and the boundless energy of children playing in neighborhood parks. Within this vibrant rhythm, the words, "Our Father in heaven, help us to honor your name," remind us to see every interaction as a chance to reflect God's holiness. Recognizing His fingerprints in our shared spaces transforms the ordinary into acts of divine grace. Honoring God's name begins with a choice to carry His love into the heart of our community. How will you shine His light in your neighborhood today?

BESIDE QUIET WATERS

A bakery's warmth comes not just from the scent of fresh bread but from the connection formed over shared stories and laughter. A library offers more than books—it becomes a sanctuary of curiosity, where neighbors inspire one another with ideas and support. Parks echo with children's laughter while parents find camaraderie in shared conversations. In these places, kindness reflects God's presence, and His love elevates the mundane to the miraculous. Choosing to nurture relationships and foster care brings honor to God's name, weaving His holiness into our everyday lives. Where can you create sacred spaces in your community?

God's vision for communities is akin to flourishing gardens, vibrant with love, service, and mutual care. Every act of kindness we extend serves as a seed planted in the rich soil of His kingdom. Over time, these seeds bear fruit, growing into a bountiful harvest of righteousness, joy, and lasting unity.

In a world that often encourages competition and isolation, God calls us to collaborate and celebrate others. Reflect His love by rejoicing in your neighbors' successes and extending help to those in need. Speak hope into a struggling heart, or generously offer your time and resources. Through intentional acts of kindness, you inspire others to seek God's grace, creating ripples that expand outward. What intentional step will you take today to show the love of Christ in your community?

RIVERS OF LIVING WATER

A woman once shared how her simple act of inviting neighbors for coffee turned into a gathering where laughter, prayer, and encouragement flowed freely. Jesus demonstrated this same intentional connection as He shared meals, taught the crowds, and prayed with His disciples. His ministry shows us that faith deepens in fellowship. In the busyness of daily life, choose moments to foster connection. Host a meal, attend a local event, or visit with a neighbor. Pray for your community, seeking opportunities to reflect God's love. Through these shared spaces, God's presence shines, and His name is honored.

The Holy Spirit draws believers together, bridging divides of language, culture, and geography. He reminds us that God's kingdom is a global family, rich in diversity but unified in purpose. This remarkable unity stands as a powerful testimony to the world of God's transformative and all-encompassing love.

Pair prayer with intentional acts of service to bring God's love to life in your community. Volunteer at a local food pantry, mentor a child, or organize a neighborhood prayer walk. Pray for local leaders and educators, asking God to guide their decisions and inspire their hearts. By combining prayer and action, you embody God's love and create a testimony of His goodness. How might your choices this week honor His name and transform your community?

DEEP CALLS TO DEEP

"Our Father in heaven, help us to honor your name." This simple yet profound prayer calls us to bring God's holiness into our shared spaces. Where division, apathy, or injustice may overshadow His light, we are invited to take small but meaningful actions to reflect His love. A kind word to a struggling neighbor, a donation to a local shelter, or simply listening to someone who feels unheard can glorify His name. Trust that God magnifies even the smallest steps of faith, transforming them into lasting ripples of grace.

Heart Prayer

Dear Heavenly Father,

Bring peace and unity to our community. May Your love heal broken hearts, mend divisions, and restore strained relationships. May every act of kindness reflect Your holiness, creating spaces where Your presence is deeply felt. Transform our neighborhoods into sanctuaries of grace and use us as vessels of Your love. Amen.

Soul Prayer

Lord Jesus,

Awaken a longing for You within our community. Build relationships that reflect Your kingdom, drawing us together in compassion and faith. Teach us to serve with humility and love boldly. May our churches and shared spaces be places of renewal, where faith is nurtured, and lives are transformed. Amen.

Mind Prayer

Holy Spirit,

Grant us wisdom to navigate the challenges of our community. Open our eyes to see the unseen and our hearts to respond with discernment. Guide our words to bring hope and healing. May our thoughts align with Your truth, creating unity and change that glorifies God. Amen.

Strength Prayer

God Three-in-One,

Empower us to serve courageously, strengthening our hands for kindness and our hearts for compassion. Help us to embody Your truth in every action. Use our efforts to bring hope and renewal to our community. May our lives glorify Your name as we work for Your kingdom.

For Thine is the kingdom, Lord Jesus
Thine is the power, Holy Spirit
And Thine is the glory, Heavenly Father,
forever. Amen.

~

Communities thrive when we step out in faith to show care and compassion. Each act of service, word of encouragement, or effort to bridge differences becomes a building block for unity. Today, ask God to show you where His love is needed in your community. Trust that your faithfulness, however small, will create lasting bonds of hope and joy.

NOTES:

DAY 4

Hallowed Be Your Name in Our State

Our Father in heaven, hallowed be
your name. (Matthew 6:9, ESV)

Our state, with its diverse landscapes, bustling cities, and serene rural areas, reminds us of God's creative power and presence. The words of the Lord's Prayer, "Our Father in heaven, hallowed be your name," invite us to honor God's holiness in every corner of our state. His majesty is reflected in rolling hills, flowing rivers, and vibrant communities. When we align our hearts with His will, seeking justice, unity, and peace, we hallow His name not only in our lives but also in the decisions and policies that shape our shared home.

BESIDE QUIET WATERS

Think about a state governed by leaders who humbly seek God's wisdom in every decision they make. Their leadership exemplifies integrity, prioritizing the welfare of all people above personal or political gain. This hopeful vision begins with our prayers and our active commitment as citizens devoted to advancing God's purposes in our communities.

God's desire for our state is rooted in the principles of His kingdom: love, justice, and humility. The Shema calls us to love Him with all our heart, soul, mind, and strength, extending that love outward into society. Picture courtrooms where impartial justice prevails, schools where children are nurtured in hope and truth, and neighborhoods built on trust and compassion. Each of us plays a role in this transformation, reflecting God's love in the way we vote, serve, and engage with one another. How can your daily actions help create a state where God's presence is evident?

The world celebrates power, wealth, and self-interest, yet God calls us to a higher path. Reflect His love by advocating for justice, supporting organizations that promote equity, and choosing integrity in all circumstances. Serve with humility and invest your time and resources in initiatives that prioritize the common good. When we act as faithful citizens of God's kingdom, we illuminate His glory in our state, creating spaces where the oppressed find freedom, the hurting find healing, and all find belonging. What will you do today to reflect His heart?

RIVERS OF LIVING WATER

Jesus demonstrated the transformative power of leadership rooted in humility and service. He challenged religious and political leaders to align with God's justice and truth. As we pray for our state, let us intercede for leaders who reflect these qualities. Ask God to guide them with wisdom, integrity, and courage as they shape policies that impact countless lives. Through prayer, we become partners in their mission to honor God's name and bring about His kingdom purposes in our communities.

The Holy Spirit equips us to pray boldly and act humbly, showing us areas where our efforts can bring lasting change. The Spirit convicts us to stand for truth, serve the vulnerable, and advocate for justice, reminding us that transformation begins in hearts surrendered to God. Trust His leadership, whether through small acts of kindness or larger initiatives. May His whispers guide you as you reflect God's love in tangible ways. How is the Spirit prompting you to make a difference in your state today?

Engage your entire being—heart, soul, mind, and strength—in prayer and service for your state. Pray fervently for leaders, educators, and communities, asking God to bring His justice and mercy to every decision and interaction. Take action by supporting local organizations, mentoring youth, or advocating for equitable policies. Use your voice and vote as tools for good, ensuring your choices align with God's love and compassion. Together, our prayers and actions can create ripples of transformation, shining Christ's light into every corner of our state.

DEEP CALLS TO DEEP

The phrase, "Hallowed be your name," calls us to surrender our state to God's will. Where injustice, division, or indifference casts shadows, we are invited to respond with faith and action. A kind word to a weary leader, participating in a community food drive, or voting with integrity can glorify God's name and bring hope to others.

As we align our lives with His purposes, we transform the heart of our state into a reflection of His kingdom.

Heart Prayer

> *Dear Heavenly Father,*
>
> *Fill our state with Your peace and replace fear with hope, division with unity. Comfort those who mourn and bring healing to the brokenhearted. May Your presence guide our leaders, inspire our communities, and transform every interaction into an opportunity for grace. Teach us to serve one another with humility and compassion, honoring Your name in all we do. May our state become a sanctuary of Your love, a place where justice prevails, and mercy flows. Amen.*

Soul Prayer

> *Lord Jesus,*
>
> *Awaken a deep longing for You across our state. Transform homes, workplaces, and communities through Your love and truth. Strengthen bonds of fellowship and inspire us to work together for the common good. Help us to live as ambassadors of Your kingdom, bringing kindness where there is strife and hope where there is despair. Use*

our lives to make Your name known and glorified. Amen.

Mind Prayer

Holy Spirit,

Grant us wisdom to navigate the complexities of our state's challenges. Help us discern Your will in difficult decisions, equipping us with clarity and courage. Guide us to speak truth with compassion and act with justice. Fill our minds with Your wisdom, and let our thoughts align with Your purposes. Through Your leading, may we reflect God's glory in every step we take. Amen.

Strength Prayer

God Three-in-One,

Empower us to serve our state with resilience, faith, and love. Strengthen us to persevere in challenges and to act boldly for Your kingdom. Help us to rely on Your grace as we extend kindness, advocate for justice, and bring hope to those in need. May our actions honor Your name and transform our communities.

For Thine is the kingdom, Lord Jesus

Thine is the power, Holy Spirit
And Thine is the glory, Heavenly Father,
forever. Amen.

~

Your state is a canvas painted with God's creative touch, from its rolling hills to its bustling cities. But beyond the landscape lies His deeper desire—for people to thrive in justice, compassion, and unity. Each prayer you lift and each act of service you offer is like a brushstroke, coloring your state with His love. Today, ask God to guide its leaders with wisdom and integrity and to use your hands and heart to bring His peace to those around you. By standing for truth, showing kindness, and living in humility, you reflect His kingdom. Trust that as you step out in faith, God is shaping your state into a testament of His grace and glory.

NOTES:

DAY 5

Hallowed Be Your Name in Our Nation

Our Father in heaven, Your name
be honored as holy.
(Matthew 6:9, HCSB)

The beauty of our nation reflects God's handiwork, from the soaring mountains to the vast plains. But even greater than the landscapes is the opportunity to cultivate unity, kindness, and faithfulness. When we honor God in our daily lives, we become stewards of this beauty, bearing witness to His grace and love.

BESIDE QUIET WATERS

A nation thrives when leaders seek God's wisdom, families honor His truth, and communities live in harmony. After the September 11 attacks, millions gathered in churches and public spaces to pray for healing and peace. These prayers reflected a collective dependence on God's guidance during a time of deep uncertainty. Consider how the power of unified prayer can shape a nation not only in crisis but as a daily act of worship. When God's name is hallowed across every sphere of society, His light shines brighter, illuminating paths of justice, compassion, and hope.

God desires our nation to be a place where His name is revered, His justice upheld, and His love reflected. Scripture says, "Blessed is the nation whose God is the Lord" (Psalm 33:12). Picture neighborhoods where kindness prevails, schools teaching values of honesty and respect, and leaders seeking divine wisdom in their decisions. Division fades as humility rises, and reconciliation thrives where God's holiness is honored. Through collective faith, our nation can reflect the kingdom of God, where His love transforms relationships, policies, and systems. This vision invites every citizen to live as a representative of His truth.

Nations often idolize power, wealth, and personal ambition, leading to corruption and division. God calls us to reflect His holiness through integrity, service, and justice. Citizens can advocate for leaders who honor His values, support initiatives that promote compassion, and pray fervently for unity. Actions like forgiving personal grievances and extending grace in public discourse reflect His name as holy. By embodying His love, individuals contribute to a national culture that aligns with His will. Let every decision, whether personal or public, hallow His name and bring His presence to the heart of the nation.

RIVERS OF LIVING WATER

Jesus embodied the essence of forgiveness, both in His teachings and through His actions. His profound act of forgiving those who nailed Him to the cross displayed the immeasurable depth of God's mercy and love. This extraordinary demonstration invites us to follow His example, extending the same boundless grace and compassion to those around us.

The Holy Spirit empowers us to embody forgiveness, equipping us to release bitterness and extend grace. He softens hardened hearts, convicts us of the need for reconciliation, and inspires us to take the first step toward peace. In the Spirit's power, families are mended, communities restored, and nations healed. As we pray for our nation, let us ask the Holy Spirit to expose areas where division persists and bring His unity. His presence equips us to live as agents of His love, seeking justice and peace. When the Spirit leads, our actions reflect His truth, allowing His name to be honored in our nation.

Pray for reconciliation within the nation by beginning with your own relationships. Extend forgiveness where division has taken root and support community initiatives that promote unity. Volunteer with organizations fostering dialogue between divided groups or serve those who feel excluded or marginalized. Personal decisions to embrace reconciliation reflect God's name as holy and invite His presence into the nation. Let God's kingdom values be evident in every action, leading to collective healing and restoration. Through prayer and service, every citizen can contribute to a unified nation that glorifies Him.

DEEP CALLS TO DEEP

The words, "Your name be honored as holy," remind us of the responsibility to reflect God's holiness in personal and national life. Identify areas where division or bitterness has taken root and ask God to guide you toward reconciliation.

Pray for national leaders to make decisions that honor God's name and for communities to seek unity over division. Small acts of service and prayer, such as volunteering or mentoring, demonstrate His care and invite His peace. Trust His ability to bring healing, and let your actions align with His call to honor His name across the nation.

Heart Prayer

Dear Heavenly Father,

Fill our nation with Your peace and heal its divisions. Guard our hearts against bitterness and teach us to forgive as You forgive us. May Your name be honored in our homes, schools, and government. Guide us to reflect Your holiness in our decisions and actions. Surround our leaders with wisdom and humility, equipping them to lead with justice and compassion. Inspire us to act as vessels of Your love, showing others that You reign in our hearts. Let our nation reflect Your kingdom, and may Your presence bring hope to every corner of our land. Amen.

Soul Prayer

Lord Jesus,

Awaken our nation to its need for Your love and guidance. Transform our hearts to reflect Your grace, fostering reconciliation in relationships and communities. Help us to align our desires with Your will and to seek Your kingdom above all else. Unite us in faith, strengthening the bonds of compassion and justice among all people. May Your Spirit move across our land, replacing pride with humility and division with peace. May our lives honor Your name as holy, shining Your light into the darkest places. Teach us to trust Your sovereignty as You guide our nation forward. Amen.

Mind Prayer

Holy Spirit,

Grant us wisdom to discern the challenges our nation faces and clarity to navigate them with truth. Teach us to see others through Your eyes, extending grace and compassion in every interaction. Equip our leaders to make decisions that reflect Your righteousness and inspire citizens to seek Your truth above all else. Protect our thoughts from divisive influences and guide our conversations with humility and kindness. May Your Word shape our minds, anchoring us in Your promises and empowering us to act with integrity. Let

*every choice honor You, bringing glory to
Your name. Amen.*

Strength Prayer

God Three-in-One,

*Strengthen us to stand for truth, justice,
and reconciliation in our nation.
Empower us to resist the temptation to
grow weary in doing good and to
persevere in promoting Your kingdom
values. Fill us with Your courage to serve
the marginalized, advocate for
righteousness, and bring healing where it
is needed most. Equip us with resilience to
overcome challenges and hope to inspire
others. May our lives reflect Your holiness,
bringing honor to Your name in every
sphere of influence. May Your power
sustain us as we shine Your light into a
broken world.*

*For Thine is the kingdom, Lord Jesus
Thine is the power, Holy Spirit
And Thine is the glory, Heavenly Father,
forever. Amen.*

~

A nation is not just defined by its borders but by the hearts
of its people. When those hearts seek God, the nation
becomes a beacon of His justice and mercy. Imagine the

power of one prayer whispered for a leader, one kind act extended to a stranger, or one voice raised for truth. These seemingly small choices weave together, creating a fabric of faith and unity. Today, lift your nation before God, asking Him to guide its leaders, heal its divisions, and inspire its citizens to reflect His love. Trust that as you live with purpose and humility, your actions will ripple outward, drawing the nation closer to the heart of His kingdom.

DAY 6

Hallowed Be Your Name in Our World

Our Father who is in heaven,
Hallowed be Your name.
(Matthew 6:9, NASB)

The vastness of our world, with its vibrant cultures, breathtaking landscapes, and intricate connections, reveals the creativity of our Creator. As we consider the words, "Our Father who is in heaven, Hallowed be Your name," let us pause to recognize God's holiness not just in our lives but across the globe. His presence is reflected in every sunrise over mountain peaks and every wave that crashes on distant shores. Each bustling market and quiet countryside whispers of His glory. His love extends to every person and every place, inviting us to honor Him not only in private devotion but in how we steward His world.

BESIDE QUIET WATERS

A small village in Rwanda, once fractured by division and hatred, stands as a living testimony to God's healing power. Years ago, this community was torn apart by violence, but the persistent prayers of a faithful few became seeds of reconciliation. Slowly, forgiveness blossomed where pain once reigned. Today, the village thrives as a symbol of hope and restoration. Stories like this remind us of God's power to transform even the most broken places. When His name is hallowed in action, the impossible becomes possible, and fractured relationships reflect His peace.

God desires our world to be a place where His love flourishes in our relationships with one another and with His creation. The Shema commands us to love God with all our heart, soul, mind, and strength (Deuteronomy 6:4–5), a love that naturally extends to the way we care for others and for the earth He has entrusted to us. Imagine a world where people celebrate their shared humanity, embracing diversity as a reflection of God's image. As we rest in His sovereignty, fear of the future diminishes. His plans for the world are good and perfect, offering a foundation of hope for every nation.

The world often encourages the pursuit of power, self-interest, and dominance over others. God calls us to a countercultural path of humility, peace, and service. We hallow His name when we advocate for justice, stand with the marginalized, and care for the earth. Choosing love over exploitation reflects His heart. From supporting policies that promote fairness to reducing waste in daily life, every decision can honor God's name. These intentional acts become declarations of His love, visible reminders of His holiness across the globe.

RIVERS OF LIVING WATER

Jesus demonstrated unwavering commitment to God's will, even when it required the ultimate sacrifice. In the garden of Gethsemane, His words— "Not my will, but yours be done" (Luke 22:42)—reflected His surrender. Kneeling in prayer, He aligned His heart with the Father's plan, trusting that His path would lead to redemption. Prayer is not about bending God's will to our desires but aligning ourselves with His purpose. As we pray for our world, let us ask for the courage to embrace His plans, even when they challenge our comfort. Like Jesus, we are invited to surrender, trusting that His ways bring life.

Through her daily prayers, a grandmother lifted her estranged family to God, hoping for reunion despite years of silence. Slowly, her unwavering faith softened hardened hearts, leading to reconciliation. This illustrates the Spirit's profound ability to mend what seems irreparable. When guided by His wisdom, even a kind word or courageous stand for justice ripples into change that reshapes lives.

Engage your heart, soul, mind, and strength in prayer and service for the world. Pray for leaders to act with wisdom and integrity, for justice to prevail, and for peace to be established. Imagine every action as a lantern shining God's light into darkness. Support efforts to alleviate poverty, protect the environment, and build bridges across cultural divides. Let Christ's love flow through your kindness, advocacy, and practical service. Each prayer and action contribute to God's renewal, reminding the world of His presence and drawing others toward His kingdom.

DEEP CALLS TO DEEP

The words, "Hallowed be Your name," as they apply to the world, invite us to consider our role in reflecting God's holiness globally. Where are the places overshadowed by injustice, conflict, or neglect that desperately need His presence? Through prayer and action, we partner with God in His work of healing and restoration. Even the smallest acts—encouraging someone in despair, planting a tree, or advocating for the vulnerable—can glorify His name. God's plans surpass human understanding, and as we surrender to Him, His love transforms not just individuals but entire nations. May we reflect His holiness boldly and faithfully.

Heart Prayer

> *Dear Heavenly Father,*
>
> *Fill our world with Your peace. Break down the walls of conflict and division, and replace them with understanding, unity, and love. Comfort those who mourn and heal the brokenhearted. Bring hope to the weary and strength to the oppressed. May Your presence be felt across every nation and among every people, and let Your name be honored in every act of reconciliation and compassion. Teach us to reflect Your heart, seeking peace and pursuing justice in a way that glorifies You. May the world become a haven of*

Your love and a reflection of Your glory. Amen.

Soul Prayer

Lord Jesus,

Awaken in the hearts of people across the world a deep longing for You. Open their eyes to see their true identity and purpose in Your love. Strengthen the bonds of community among cultures and nations, showing us how to support one another in our spiritual journeys. Let faith flourish in every corner of the globe, bringing hope where despair has reigned. Help us to be Your hands and feet, serving with joy and humility. Let every nation hear of Your name and respond with praise, transforming the world into a reflection of Your kingdom. Amen.

Mind Prayer

Holy Spirit,

Grant us wisdom as we confront the challenges facing our world. Help us to see through Your eyes, recognizing the dignity in every person and the beauty of creation. Teach us to think with clarity and to respond with compassion to the needs of others. Fill our minds with Your truth and guide our decisions to align with Your will. Equip us to speak words of kindness and justice that honor Your name and inspire hope. Lead us to creative solutions that foster unity, peace, and renewal across the globe. May our thoughts and actions reflect Your love. Amen.

Strength Prayer

God Three-in-One,

Empower us to serve with boldness and humility, bringing Your love to the world through our words and actions. Grant us the strength to face challenges with perseverance and faith. Help us to embody Your truth, offering compassion to the hurting and hope to the discouraged. Give us courage to stand for justice and resilience to keep walking in obedience when the path is difficult. Use our lives as instruments of Your grace, transforming the world for Your glory. May every step we take honor Your name and reflect Your kingdom on earth.

For Thine is the kingdom, Lord Jesus
Thine is the power, Holy Spirit
And Thine is the glory, Heavenly Father,

forever. Amen.

~

God calls us to join Him in His work of renewal, both near and far. Through prayer, generosity, and compassion, we reflect on His heart for the world. Today, focus on how you can uplift someone beyond your immediate circle—whether by supporting a global cause, praying for peace, or showing kindness to a stranger. Trust that God will use your faithfulness to bring hope and healing in ways you may not yet see.

NOTES:

DAY 7

Thy Kingdom Come in Our Home

Thy kingdom come, Thy will be done in earth, as it is in heaven.
(Matthew 6:10, KJV)

The sacred space of our homes, where love and daily life intertwine, holds a unique potential for God's kingdom to flourish. The words, "Thy kingdom come, Thy will be done in earth, as it is in heaven," remind us that His transformative presence begins within our walls. Family life is a beautiful yet challenging journey, filled with moments of laughter and trials of patience. God's kingdom is not a distant dream but a reality waiting to unfold in our homes. Just as a mustard seed grows into a mighty tree, homes where faith takes root can become places of flourishing love and enduring peace.

BESIDE QUIET WATERS

The Garcia family, whose home hums with the energy of three children, provides a vivid glimpse into this truth. Their days are punctuated by bursts of laughter and the gentle clatter of toys, mingling with the aroma of home-cooked meals. Yet, their home also bears the marks of conflict—moments of bickering over toys and the frayed patience that comes with exhaustion. By choosing to embrace God's kingdom, the Garcias turn these struggles into opportunities for grace. A whispered apology, a forgiving hug, or a prayerful pause between chores reflects their commitment to unity. Though imperfect, they model how daily surrender to God's will transforms even chaotic homes into sanctuaries of love.

God desires every home to reflect His kingdom, where relationships are healed and strengthened by His presence. The Shema calls us to love Him with all our heart, soul, mind, and strength—a love meant to overflow into how we speak, act, and serve. Homes built on this foundation radiate peace and invite God into every decision and conversation. Faith fuels forgiveness, gratitude replaces grumbling, and love overcomes selfishness. Imagine a family meal filled with laughter and encouragement or a living room where prayer becomes the heartbeat of togetherness. These small yet profound moments shape homes into reflections of God's kingdom.

God's kingdom calls us to resist the world's lure of prioritizing self-interest, material success, or superficial appearances. Homes centered on His love choose a higher path. Speak life into your family by offering encouragement instead of criticism. Find joy in small acts of kindness like preparing a favorite meal or lending a listening ear. Build your home on the unshakable foundation of His Word, finding strength in His promises during trials. May His peace fill your heart as you navigate the challenges of family life, knowing that each choice to reflect His love draws others closer to His light. How might the rhythms of your home change if each moment became an opportunity to cultivate God's kingdom?

RIVERS OF LIVING WATER

Jesus often illustrated God's kingdom through parables about seeds and soil, teaching us that persistent prayer nourishes the spiritual ground of our homes. Seeds of faith, watered with Scripture and nurtured with love, grow into lives anchored in His presence. Prayer becomes the steady rhythm of a home, sustaining it with God's grace. Picture a family bowing their heads before dinner, a bedtime prayer whispered by a tired child, or a spontaneous moment of gratitude in the middle of a hectic day. These habits, though simple, cultivate an environment where faith thrives, and the kingdom of God grows stronger with each act of devotion.

The Holy Spirit strengthens us to persevere in prayer, even when answers seem delayed. His presence assures us that unseen growth is taking place, softening hardened hearts and replacing tension with peace. When the Garcias faced financial strain, their prayers became more than requests—they became lifelines. As they prayed, God revealed areas in need of surrender, prompting forgiveness and trust. Prayer not only transformed their circumstances but also aligned their hearts with His will. Each moment of prayer is like a seed planted by the unseen gardener, who faithfully nurtures growth in His time. Trust that He is working, even in silence.

Prayer engages every part of who we are—heart, soul, mind, and strength—and transforms our homes when woven into daily life. Create a rhythm of shared prayers that include grace before meals, bedtime blessings, and spontaneous intercessions for one another. Speak words of life into your home and let forgiveness flow freely. When interruptions arise, seize them as opportunities to reflect Christ's patience. Serve one another with joy, knowing these acts mirror His humility. Let every interaction, no matter how ordinary, become an offering of worship. As God's kingdom takes root in your family, the Spirit will illuminate your home with peace and unity.

DEEP CALLS TO DEEP

The words, "Thy kingdom come," invite deep reflection on God's presence in your home. Relationships, routines, and attitudes can reflect His reign when surrendered to His will. Imagine a child offering an unprompted apology, a parent speaking encouragement in the face of frustration, or a family choosing prayer over argument. Such moments, though small, usher in the kingdom of God. Consider whether there are areas where you've resisted surrendering control or relationships that need healing. Trust that God's presence transforms hearts and homes, making them reflections of His peace. How might small acts of faith—like offering forgiveness or listening with patience—open the door for His kingdom today?

Heart Prayer

Dear Heavenly Father,

Fill our home with Your peace. Replace conflict with harmony and division with understanding. Teach us to forgive as You forgive us and to love each other deeply. Comfort the hurting and heal broken relationships. Let every corner of our home reflect Your kingdom and radiate Your grace. Amen.

Soul Prayer

Lord Jesus,

Reveal Your purpose for each member of our household. Help us find identity and worth in Your love, not the world's opinion. Teach us to serve one another with joy and humility, reflecting Your selfless example. Unite us as a family, rooted in Your truth and bound by Your grace. Amen.

Mind Prayer

Holy Spirit,

Guide us as we navigate the challenges of family life. Help us make decisions aligned with Your truth. Protect us from distractions and grant us wisdom to prioritize what honors You. Fill our minds with peace and clarity so that our choices glorify You. Amen.

Strength Prayer

God Three-in-One,

Strengthen us to face trials with resilience and grace. Empower us to love selflessly and serve faithfully. Anchor our hearts in Your presence and sustain us with Your love. May our home shine as a shining light of Your peace and truth.

For Thine is the kingdom, Lord Jesus
Thine is the power, Holy Spirit
And Thine is the glory, Heavenly Father,
forever. Amen.

~

The foundation of God's kingdom begins within the walls of your home. Each merciful word spoken, prayer shared, and act of forgiveness offered creates an environment where His presence thrives. Picture a family choosing love over conflict, patience over frustration, and faith over fear. These moments, though small, become transformative when surrendered to Him. Today, invite God to guide your family, shaping your home into a place where His peace dwells and His truth takes root. Whether through a prayer before a meal or a conversation that brings reconciliation, trust that He is working to align your home with the values of His kingdom, one faithful step at a time.

DAY 8

Thy Kingdom Come in Our Neighborhood

Your kingdom come, your will be done, on earth as it is in heaven. (Matthew 6:10, NIV)

The vibrant fabric of our neighborhoods holds limitless potential for reflecting God's kingdom. The words, "Your kingdom come, your will be done," call us to look at our streets with fresh eyes. Every passerby, every neighbor, and even the stranger we meet in daily routines is a divine appointment waiting to unfold. These encounters are not mere coincidences but sacred opportunities to extend God's transformative love. When we greet someone warmly, share a meal, or lend a helping hand, we weave threads of heaven into the everyday, showing others what it means to live in step with God's heart.

BESIDE QUIET WATERS

After a fire destroyed the Johnson family's home, their neighborhood rallied together to meet their needs. Neighbors brought warm meals, provided clothing, and raised funds to help the family rebuild. Among them was Mrs. Larkin, a widow who lived on a modest income. She contributed what little she could—a knitted blanket and jars of homemade preserves—offering not only comfort but also hope. Her selfless love echoed the faithfulness of Ruth, whose kindness transformed Naomi's despair. Mrs. Larkin's small yet heartfelt actions planted seeds of unity, reminding everyone that God's kingdom flourishes where sacrificial love takes root.

God envisions our neighborhoods as reflections of His kingdom, where love overflows and relationships thrive. The Shema calls us to love God with all our heart, soul, mind, and strength, and this love must extend outward into our communities. Imagine streets filled with laughter, where differences are celebrated and struggles shared. Picture neighbors gathering on porches, children playing without fear, and burdens carried together in faith. These glimpses of heaven are possible when we invite the Holy Spirit to lead us in sowing seeds of peace, trust, and compassion. Through small yet intentional acts, we can turn ordinary streets into sacred spaces where God's glory shines.

The world often teaches us to isolate ourselves, prioritize convenience, and live behind walls of privacy. God, however, calls us to open our doors and our hearts. Offer help to a struggling neighbor, extend forgiveness where tension has lingered, and pray over the houses on your street. Choose to reflect His kingdom by welcoming the overlooked, serving the brokenhearted, and speaking life into weary souls. Every act of love declares His presence and invites His power to transform. Through these simple steps, we tear down barriers and build bridges of grace, creating neighborhoods where God's will is done on earth as it is in heaven.

RIVERS OF LIVING WATER

When Jesus told the parable of the Good Samaritan, He challenged us to rethink what it means to love our neighbor. His story reminds us that neighbors aren't defined by proximity but by opportunity—anyone in need is someone God has placed in our path. Prayer is the foundation for loving well, turning our hearts toward those who are hurting. Begin by lifting up the needs of your neighbors, asking God to guide your words and actions. Whether it's through a kind gesture, a listening ear, or a shared celebration, each interaction becomes a chance to reveal God's kingdom.

The Holy Spirit empowers us to love with a depth that transcends barriers of culture, class, or convenience. Through His prompting, we see others as God sees them— worthy of dignity, care, and compassion. Imagine a quiet nudge from the Spirit leading you to check on a lonely neighbor or offer a meal to a family in need. These small steps often open doors to reconciliation and healing. Mrs. Larkin shared how her simple act of knitting a blanket for the Johnson family rekindled her own faith. Trust that the Spirit is already at work in your neighborhood, calling you to join in His redemptive plan.

Dedicate your heart, soul, mind, and strength to prayer and action. Greet the stranger who often walks alone past your house. Leave a handwritten note of encouragement for a neighbor who may be struggling. As you stroll your neighborhood, pray for the families behind each door, asking God to bring peace, unity, and joy to their lives. Organize a block party or invite neighbors for a meal, creating space for connections to grow. These intentional acts—rooted in prayer and kindness—create ripples of God's grace, transforming ordinary streets into places where His love is unmistakable.

DEEP CALLS TO DEEP

The words, "Your kingdom come," are an invitation to see our neighborhoods through God's eyes. Are there fences needing mending or wounds requiring healing? Are there needs overlooked because of our busyness? Transformation begins with prayer, but it is fulfilled through action. A kind smile to the mail carrier, a loaf of bread delivered to a new family, or simply taking time to listen to a neighbor's story can sow seeds of faith that ripple outward. Surrender your neighborhood to God's purposes, trusting Him to magnify your smallest acts of love. Each step of faith reflects His kingdom and makes His presence tangible.

Heart Prayer

Dear Heavenly Father,

Fill our neighborhoods with Your peace and unity. Where division and fear have taken root, plant seeds of love and trust.

Teach us to love deeply, serve compassionately, and celebrate each other's victories. May every interaction reflect Your presence, and may our streets become sanctuaries where Your name is glorified. Amen.

Soul Prayer

Lord Jesus,

Awaken a longing for You in our neighbors' hearts. Strengthen our bonds of community, teaching us to value relationships over convenience. Use us to reflect the beauty of Your kingdom, bringing hope, joy, and restoration. May every word and action mirror Your love, inspiring others to seek You. Amen.

Mind Prayer

Holy Spirit,

Grant us wisdom to see and respond to the needs around us. Help us to speak words of life and encouragement, bringing light into moments of despair. May our thoughts align with Your truth and may every decision we make glorify God's name. Teach us to love with discernment and humility. Amen.

Strength Prayer

God Three-in-One,

Empower us to serve boldly and joyfully in our neighborhoods. Give us courage to step into challenging spaces and compassion to meet others' needs. Let our actions reflect Your truth and transform our streets into shining lights of Your light. Sustain us with Your strength as we work to bring Your kingdom closer to earth.

For Thine is the kingdom, Lord Jesus
Thine is the power, Holy Spirit
And Thine is the glory, Heavenly Father,
forever. Amen.

~

Your neighborhood is a space where God's love can flourish through intentional connections. Each act of kindness—whether through a warm conversation, an offer to help, or a prayer—brings His peace closer to home. Today, reflect on how you can create moments of unity and care for those around you. Trust that your steps of faith will build a community that reflects His grace.

NOTES:

DAY 9

Thy Kingdom Come in Our Community

*Come and set up your kingdom, so
that everyone on earth will obey
you, as you are obeyed in heaven.
(Matthew 6:10, CEV)*

Communities are the sacred heart of connection, where lives are intertwined, stories are shared, and redemption becomes tangible. The words of the Lord's Prayer, "Come and set up your kingdom, so that everyone on earth will obey you, as you are obeyed in heaven," invite us to live under the banner of His purpose. God's kingdom emerges when we extend His kindness, justice, and forgiveness to one another in ways that are both bold and gentle. The smallest acts—like offering a smile or extending a helping hand—have the power to transform shared spaces into sanctuaries of hope, healing, and belonging.

BESIDE QUIET WATERS

In a town deeply impacted by economic inequality, a devoted church began a mentoring program for children attending underfunded schools. This program offered more than academic support; it fostered self-esteem and cultivated values such as integrity and perseverance. Over time, the initiative grew into a beacon of hope, illustrating the transformative power of faith communities to heal societal divides through compassion and purposeful action.

God envisions communities where love, justice, and mercy are not ideals but lived realities. His command to love Him fully and serve others calls us to imagine neighborhoods teeming with kindness, schools championing respect and integrity, and leaders acting with humility. Picture the hurting finding healing, the marginalized discovering belonging, and despair being overtaken by joy. God's kingdom thrives when His people live in obedience, surrendering personal ambition to serve others selflessly. As followers of Christ, we are called to make this vision tangible in the communities we call home, letting His light shine through us.

Worldly priorities often elevate individual success above collective unity. God's call is different. He asks us to reverse this trend by reflecting His love and advocating for His justice. Hallowing His name means building relationships that embody His values—mentoring struggling youth, feeding the hungry, and investing in community initiatives that heal and restore. Imagine prayer circles forming in places once marked by division or neighbors gathering for acts of reconciliation. When we choose to act on His word, communities begin to mirror heaven, and His kingdom becomes evident in both quiet gestures and bold actions.

RIVERS OF LIVING WATER

Jesus' ministry demonstrates how acts of compassion become living testimonies of God's kingdom. When He restored Zacchaeus, healed the lepers, or spoke with the Samaritan woman, He revealed that no one is beyond the reach of His grace. Prayer played a vital role in this work— not just personal prayer, but intercession for others. Communities grow stronger when God's people pray boldly, lifting up leaders, neighbors, and the vulnerable. Intercessory prayer creates an open door for His presence to bring healing and unity. Imagine a neighborhood where every prayer becomes a seed, planted for the flourishing of God's will.

The Holy Spirit moves through believers to bring God's kingdom into focus. His presence inspires us to forgive, confront injustice with grace, and build bridges where there were once divides. Communities are transformed when His guidance leads us to serve as peacemakers and ambassadors of love. In one instance, a grandmother's prayers for her estranged family eventually softened hearts, leading to reconciliation and healing. Such is the Spirit's power—to mend what seems irreparably broken. When we trust His leading, even small acts of love, like offering an encouraging word or standing up for what is right, ripple into lasting change.

Living as an ambassador of God's kingdom requires both prayer and action. Engage with community needs by advocating for equitable policies, volunteering at food banks, or participating in local outreach. Love shines brightest when paired with listening—hearing the stories of neighbors and responding with care. Imagine a gathering where walls of misunderstanding fall away, replaced by genuine connection. When forgiveness replaces resentment and service overcomes apathy, the community becomes fertile ground for God's work. Let your actions reflect His grace, ensuring others see His heart through the kindness you show and the prayers you lift.

DEEP CALLS TO DEEP

The words, "Come and set up your kingdom," urge us to see our communities through God's eyes. Where are the broken relationships or neglected needs where His kingdom could take root? Strained ties, systemic injustices, or overlooked neighbors become opportunities for God's mercy and justice to break through. Simple acts like mentoring, advocating for fairness, or volunteering invite His presence into our shared spaces. Trust in His ability to multiply the impact of your efforts. When surrendered to Him, even the smallest gestures become catalysts for change, creating ripples that extend far beyond what we can imagine.

Heart Prayer

Dear Heavenly Father,

Transform our communities with Your peace, replacing fear with unity and division with love. Teach us to see neighbors as Your children, worthy of compassion and dignity. May Your presence heal wounds caused by neglect or misunderstanding and inspire acts of service that reflect Your grace. Guard our hearts against bitterness and selfishness, enabling us to forgive freely and love generously. May Your kingdom values shape every corner of our community, bringing hope to the broken and strength to the weary. May Your name be glorified through lives surrendered to Your will. Amen.

Soul Prayer

Lord Jesus,

Awaken in our neighborhoods a longing for Your love and truth. Unite our community in faith, breaking down walls of division and replacing them with reconciliation. Strengthen families and friendships, build a network of care and support that reflects Your kingdom. Show us how to uplift those who feel forgotten, meeting their needs with humility and compassion. Transform our souls to seek Your purpose above our own, aligning our lives with Your holy will. May our communities reflect Your light, drawing others to Your peace and love. Inspire us to live boldly for Your kingdom. Amen.

Mind Prayer

Holy Spirit,

Grant us wisdom to address the challenges facing our communities with clarity and truth. Help us to see others through Your eyes, extending compassion where there is pain and empathy where there is misunderstanding. Equip our leaders to govern with justice and integrity and inspire citizens to act with kindness and courage. Protect our thoughts from division and discouragement and fill us with Your hope and perspective. May Your Word shape our minds, anchoring us in Your promises and directing our steps toward unity. Use our voices to speak truth and love, building a community that honors You. Amen.

Strength Prayer

God Three-in-One,

Strengthen us to live out Your love in practical ways, facing trials with courage and grace. Teach us to depend on Your power, serving with humility and offering forgiveness freely. Equip us to persevere in difficult times and to shine Your light in places of darkness. May Your Spirit sustain us as we extend kindness and support to those in need. Transform our communities through Your strength, creating havens of peace and unity. May Your power inspire acts of love that reflect Your kingdom and honor Your holy name. Use us to bring Your presence into every corner.

For Thine is the kingdom, Lord Jesus
Thine is the power, Holy Spirit
And Thine is the glory, Heavenly Father,
forever. Amen.

~

Communities thrive when love and faith intertwine in daily actions. Imagine a gathering place where forgiveness replaces resentment, generosity meets need, and shared purpose fosters unity. God calls us to make this vision a reality, beginning with simple choices—supporting a local effort, mentoring a young soul, or offering a heartfelt prayer for those around you. Today, reflect His love by stepping into a need you see, however small. Trust that each act of kindness is like a seed planted in fertile soil, and God will nurture it into growth that brings hope, healing, and His presence into every corner of your community.

NOTES:

DAY 10

Thy Kingdom Come in Our State

Your kingdom come, your will be
done, on earth as it is in heaven.
(Matthew 6:10, ESV)

Communities large and small form the intricate fabric of our state, where every choice made within them ripples outward, shaping lives in ways we cannot always see. The prayer, "Your kingdom come, your will be done, on earth as it is in heaven," invites us to align our hearts, actions, and values with God's purposes. His kingdom takes root when love replaces division, when justice uplifts the downtrodden, and when mercy transforms hardened hearts. This prayer is not for an abstract ideal but for a living, breathing reality—one that grows where faith meets action. As we surrender our interactions and decisions to His will, God's transformative presence begins to shape our state into a reflection of heaven's priorities.

The story of a state senator who expressed his faith through dedicated public service is a compelling example of living out God's principles. Advocating for the voiceless and championing justice, he brought the values of God's kingdom to life in practical and impactful ways. His unwavering commitment to God's calling continues to inspire others to blend faith with meaningful action.

BESIDE QUIET WATERS

Imagine a state where every action, from a teacher's encouragement to a leader's just decision, echoes God's kingdom. His vision calls us to reflect His love in civic life, relationships, and daily choices. A classroom that nurtures both truth and compassion, or a workplace shaped by fairness, becomes a testament to His guidance. As His people align with His will, our state transforms into a shining light of hope and renewal, embodying Mark 12:30's call to love God fully.

The world often celebrates power, self-interest, and convenience at the expense of fairness and integrity. God calls us to a higher standard. His people are to seek justice, embrace mercy, and walk humbly with Him in every sphere of life. Advocating for policies that uplift the marginalized, volunteering in efforts that serve the needy, and building relationships grounded in truth are ways to reflect His kingdom values. A single act of kindness—a thoughtful word, a shared meal, or a prayer for a neighbor—becomes a seed of transformation. Together, these seeds grow into a state where God's will is not only visible but celebrated.

RIVERS OF LIVING WATER

Jesus modeled boldness in confronting systems of corruption and injustice, calling leaders to align their actions with God's righteousness. His teachings challenge us to pray for those in authority with humility, asking God to guide their hearts and decisions. Communities flourish when leadership is undergirded by prayer, aligning priorities with God's vision. His words, "Your will be done," remind us to intercede for wisdom, courage, and compassion for those shaping our state's future. Imagine the ripple effects of heartfelt prayers, lifting leaders' burdens and opening doors for God's kingdom to influence even the most complex systems.

The Holy Spirit moves through us, equipping believers to act and pray with purpose. His presence convicts hearts and leads communities toward reconciliation and righteousness. A grandmother's fervent prayers once mended the divide within her fractured family. Over time, bitterness gave way to peace, and estranged relationships were restored. In the same way, God can use our intercession to bring unity and healing to our state. Imagine a state where leaders and citizens alike seek His wisdom, where neighbors foster understanding, and where communities stand united in love. Through the Spirit's guidance, believers can address injustice with grace and courage, transforming hearts and institutions.

Prayer and action are inseparable companions in the pursuit of God's purposes. Through prayer, we align our hearts with His will, seeking His guidance and strength. By stepping into action, we bring His love into the world, making our faith both visible and transformative for those around us.

DEEP CALLS TO DEEP

The prayer, "Your kingdom come," invites us to surrender our state to God's reign. Where do you see the need for His justice, love, and truth? Relationships broken by division, policies rooted in self-interest, and communities burdened by inequity are fertile ground for His kingdom to take root. Simple acts—mentoring, volunteering, or advocating for fairness—become the seeds of transformation when offered in faith. Trust that God magnifies even the smallest steps of obedience, creating ripples that extend far beyond what we can imagine. Commit your prayers and actions to Him, and watch as His kingdom transforms every aspect of our state.

Heart Prayer

> *Dear Heavenly Father,*
>
> *Fill our state with Your peace, replacing fear with unity and division with love. Guard our leaders against corruption and inspire them to pursue justice. Teach us to extend grace to neighbors and forgiveness to those who hurt us. May Your compassion move us to act, transforming our communities into reflections of Your kingdom. Help us to see the needs around us and respond with courage and kindness. May Your name be glorified as we serve*

with humility and trust in Your guidance. Let our state reflect Your heart for justice and mercy. Amen.

Soul Prayer

Lord Jesus,

Awaken our state to its need for Your truth and love. Teach us to embody Your compassion as we advocate for the vulnerable and unite communities in peace. Strengthen bonds within neighborhoods and among leaders, creating networks of care that reflect Your kingdom. Show us how to mend divisions and promote reconciliation. Transform our souls to seek Your will above personal ambition, aligning every action with Your purpose. May our state become a shining light of hope, where Your light shines through relationships and initiatives inspired by Your love. Inspire us to live boldly for Your glory. Amen.

Mind Prayer

Holy Spirit,

Grant wisdom to our leaders as they navigate challenges and opportunities. Teach citizens to discern truth and to advocate for policies that reflect Your justice and compassion. Guard our minds against fear and division, replacing negativity with trust in Your promises. Shape our perspectives to prioritize unity and understanding. Equip us to approach community issues with creativity and collaboration. Anchor our thoughts in Your truth, inspiring actions that align with Your kingdom. Guide us to use our voices for good, encouraging others to seek Your will. Amen.

Strength Prayer

God Three-in-One,

Empower us to serve our state with resilience and love, persevering in the face of challenges. Strengthen us to speak truth, extend grace, and promote justice in every sphere of influence. Help us to rely on Your power as we seek to bring Your kingdom values into our communities. Teach us to act boldly in faith, trusting in Your guidance and provision. May Your presence transform our state, renewing it with hope and unity. May every effort we make honor Your name and reflect Your glory. Use us to build a state where Your love reigns.

For Thine is the kingdom, Lord Jesus
Thine is the power, Holy Spirit
And Thine is the glory, Heavenly Father,
forever. Amen.

~

A state is shaped not just by its leaders but by the collective heart of its people. Imagine schools where truth and compassion guide learning, neighborhoods where kindness overcomes division, and workplaces where integrity shapes every decision. God calls us to be part of this transformation by living out His love in our daily actions. Today, pray for wisdom for your state's leaders, extend a hand to someone in need, or stand for justice in your corner of influence. Trust that your faithfulness, no matter how small, contributes to His greater work of renewal, turning ordinary moments into glimpses of His kingdom at work.

NOTES:

DAY 11

Thy Kingdom Come in Our Nation

*Your kingdom come. Your will be
done on earth as it is in heaven.
(Matthew 6:10, HCSB)*

The words of Jesus' prayer, "Your kingdom come. Your will
be done on earth as it is in heaven," remind us that God
invites us into His redemptive work. Across the vast
expanse of our nation—with its diverse cultures, voices,
and challenges—we are called to reflect the values of His
kingdom. This prayer is a call to embody His justice,
mercy, and compassion in every sphere of life. When His
kingdom takes root, healing replaces brokenness, peace
dispels division, and unity triumphs over discord. God's
vision for our nation begins not in grand gestures, but in
the quiet surrender of our hearts and the faithful steps we
take to mirror His love.

BESIDE QUIET WATERS

A nation where righteousness defines its laws, and compassion shapes its policies reflects the heart of God. A judge once revolutionized his city's justice system by introducing restorative justice programs that offered mentorship and second chances to offenders. Through this work, lives were changed, and a community divided by despair began to rebuild. Similarly, during the abolitionist movement, ordinary people came together to challenge oppression and create a society rooted in freedom and equality. These stories remind us that when we live out kingdom principles, profound transformation occurs. Imagine a nation where such stories become the norm—a place where mercy heals wounds, and justice uplifts the oppressed.

God longs for our nation to reflect His kingdom, where love is expressed through justice, compassion, and mercy. Scripture teaches us to love Him with all our heart, soul, mind, and strength, a love that overflows into the way we live, serve, and lead. Picture a nation united in its commitment to care for the vulnerable and uplift the downtrodden. Schools filled with encouragement, neighborhoods thriving with kindness, and leaders who govern with integrity all reflect His will. This vision requires our participation, choosing His priorities over personal comfort and embodying His love in every action.

The world often elevates self-interest, power, and material gain over integrity and fairness. God calls us to a higher standard: to walk humbly with Him and seek justice in every decision. Advocacy for just policies, intentional acts of kindness, and compassionate conversations reveal His love in practical ways. Choosing to honor His name requires small, consistent steps of faith, trusting that these actions create ripples of transformation. May we embrace this calling to hallow His name, trusting that He can use our faithfulness to shape a nation that reflects His heart.

RIVERS OF LIVING WATER

Jesus' life and ministry consistently prioritized the values of God's kingdom. His teaching challenged followers to seek eternal purposes over fleeting ambitions. His example compels us to do the same, trusting God's wisdom and praying for His justice to reign. During His time on earth, Jesus taught us to pray, "Your will be done," emphasizing alignment with God's heart. Imagine a nation where every prayer becomes a foundation for decisions, aligning leaders and communities with God's truth. May we lift up our nation in prayer, confident that God is faithful to transform hearts and systems for His glory.

The Holy Spirit equips believers with wisdom and courage to engage in God's redemptive work. He prompts us to see needs we might otherwise overlook and empowers us to take action. A woman in her local community once felt led to organize a pantry that provided food for struggling families. Her single act of obedience sparked a movement, creating a ripple of hope and healing across her city. Transformation often begins with small, Spirit-led steps of faith that God multiplies for His purposes. Trust Him to guide your prayers and actions as we reflect His kingdom in our nation.

Engage your heart, soul, mind, and strength in God's work. Begin by praying for leaders, asking God to grant them discernment and integrity. Look for opportunities to serve your community, whether by mentoring youth, volunteering at shelters, or advocating for policies that reflect God's justice. Faithful actions—no matter how small—become shining lights of His light. Imagine a nation where God's presence is visible through acts of reconciliation, compassion, and service. Together, through prayer and action, we can help bring His kingdom on earth as it is in heaven.

DEEP CALLS TO DEEP

God calls us to pray boldly for our nation, trusting Him to guide and transform. The words, "Your kingdom come," challenge us to consider how we can align our actions with His purposes. Where do you see the need for His justice and love? Are there broken systems or communities waiting for healing? Through acts of obedience—mentoring a struggling youth, advocating for fairness, or organizing a local prayer walk—we create ripples of change that extend beyond our view. Trust that God's power magnifies every step of faith, bringing His kingdom into places longing for hope.

Heart Prayer

Dear Heavenly Father,

Fill our nation with Your peace, replacing fear with unity and division with love. Comfort those who grieve and heal broken relationships that hinder understanding. Teach us to reflect Your love in our words and actions, showing kindness even to those who oppose us. Bless our leaders with wisdom and integrity, inspiring them to make decisions that honor You. May Your presence fill every corner of our nation, transforming communities into reflections of Your grace and truth. May we honor Your name in all we do, becoming instruments of Your justice and mercy. Amen.

Soul Prayer

Lord Jesus,

Awaken our nation to its need for Your truth and love. Reconcile division and foster relationships that reflect Your kingdom values. Strengthen the bonds of community, teaching us to serve one another in humility and faith. Show us how to reflect Your love boldly, creating spaces where grace and restoration thrive. May Your truth guide our desires, and may our actions honor Your holy name. May our nation become a shining light of Your hope and healing, drawing others toward Your light and glory. Inspire us to follow Your example. Amen.

Mind Prayer

Holy Spirit,

Grant us wisdom to navigate the complexities of our nation. Protect our minds from fear and confusion, filling us with understanding and discernment. Teach us to see others with compassion, offering encouragement and solutions that align with Your truth. Inspire our leaders and citizens to act with justice and integrity. May Your Word guide our thoughts, shaping decisions that honor Your name and uplift others. Equip us to use our voices for unity, and may every action reflect Your kingdom. Let our minds align with Your promises, creating a foundation for transformation. Amen.

Strength Prayer

God Three-in-One,

Strengthen us to persevere in love and service. Empower us to stand for justice, offering hope to the discouraged and advocacy for the vulnerable. Teach us to trust in Your power rather than our own, relying on Your grace in every challenge. May Your Spirit sustain us as we work to reflect Your kingdom in practical ways.

Transform our nation through acts of love, reconciliation, and faith. May Your kingdom come, and Your will be done in every act of courage and kindness. May Your name be glorified in all we do.

For Thine is the kingdom, Lord Jesus
Thine is the power, Holy Spirit
And Thine is the glory, Heavenly Father,
forever. Amen.

~

A nation grounded in God's love becomes a place where hearts are transformed and hope flourishes. Imagine leaders seeking His wisdom, communities united in compassion, and families strengthened by His peace. Each prayer lifted for your nation and each choice to act justly contributes to this transformation. Today, ask God to guide those in authority, to heal divisions, and to inspire citizens to reflect His love in every decision. Whether through offering forgiveness, standing for truth, or serving someone in need, trust that your faith will ripple outward. Together, our small steps of faith can align a nation with His eternal purposes and His unshakable kingdom.

NOTES:

DAY 12

Thy Kingdom Come in Our World

*Your kingdom come. Your will be
done, On earth as it is in heaven.
(Matthew 6:10, NASB)*

The diversity and complexity of our world reveal both its
breathtaking beauty and its deep brokenness, drawing us
to reflect on Jesus' prayer: "Your kingdom come. Your will
be done, On earth as it is in heaven." This plea is not a
passive hope but an urgent call to align our hearts and
actions with God's redemptive work. His kingdom is not
confined to heaven's perfection but actively breaks into
our world through surrendered lives. Every choice to love
instead of hate, to seek peace instead of sowing discord,
and to serve instead of seeking self-interest becomes a
conduit for His kingdom to take root in tangible ways.

BESIDE QUIET WATERS

In a bustling marketplace in Marrakech, the vibrant hum of voices mingles with the rich aromas of spices and food stalls. Amid the chaos, a boy named Omar extends a cup of water to a weary traveler—a small yet profound act that mirrors the heart of God's kingdom. On the other side of the globe, a ministry in the slums of Rio de Janeiro equips children with education and mentorship, planting seeds of hope where despair once reigned. Similarly, the legacy of William Carey's missionary work in India reminds us of the far-reaching impact of one life fully committed to God's purposes. These moments reveal that every act of love, no matter how small, carries eternal significance when done for Him.

God envisions a world where His kingdom values—justice, mercy, and unity—permeate every nation and culture. His desire is for governments to reflect His justice, for communities to embrace His mercy, and for individuals to extend His compassion. The Shema calls us to love God with all our heart, soul, mind, and strength, and this love must overflow into the global community. Imagine a world where leaders govern with humility, citizens prioritize the welfare of others, and nations thrive in His peace. This vision is not simply an ideal; it is an invitation to live as His ambassadors.

The world often prioritizes power, material wealth, and self-interest over equity and justice. God calls us to reject these pursuits and instead walk humbly, love mercy, and act justly. This may mean volunteering with global charities, supporting fair-trade initiatives, or advocating for systemic change through letters or petitions. Each action—no matter how small—becomes a prayer in motion, hallowing His name. Faith that acts boldly, compassion that crosses boundaries, and courage that refuses to shrink from hard conversations reveal His kingdom to a world desperately in need of hope.

RIVERS OF LIVING WATER

In the Garden of Gethsemane, Jesus prayed with ultimate surrender, "Not my will, but Yours, be done." His obedience opened the path to salvation and modeled the courage required to align with God's purposes. This same call invites us to face global challenges such as human trafficking, systemic poverty, and climate change with faith, trusting His vision over our limited understanding. True surrender does not demand control but trusts the One who holds the future. When we align our prayers and actions with His will, His kingdom begins to heal and restore the brokenness around us.

The Holy Spirit equips believers with the wisdom to navigate the world's complexities. Through Him, our prayers align with God's heart, and our actions carry His power. A missionary once felt a Spirit-led prompting to establish a small clinic in a war-torn region. Though her resources were limited, her faith unlocked opportunities for hundreds to receive medical care and hope. Transformation begins with small steps of obedience sustained by God's strength. Trust the Spirit to guide your heart, leading you to be His hands and feet in places that most need His love and justice.

Engage every part of your being—heart, soul, mind, and strength—in God's work. Start by lifting global leaders in prayer, asking for integrity and compassion in their decisions. Partner with international charities, sponsor children, or volunteer with organizations that reflect God's kingdom values. Consider joining or supporting local prayer groups that intercede for global issues. Each act of faith, from the smallest prayer to the boldest action, becomes a seed in God's redemptive plan, carrying His justice and mercy to the farthest reaches of the earth.

DEEP CALLS TO DEEP

God invites us to pray boldly for the broken places in our world, trusting His power to bring healing and redemption. The words, "Your kingdom come," challenge us to align our actions with His purposes, even when the work seems overwhelming. Reflect on areas where His presence is desperately needed—war zones, underserved communities, or the halls of power—and consider how you can serve as His hands and feet. Whether mentoring a struggling youth or supporting global initiatives for justice, trust that God multiplies even the smallest acts of faith, creating ripples of transformation across the globe.

Heart Prayer

> *Dear Heavenly Father,*
>
> *Fill our world with Your peace, replacing fear with trust and division with unity. Comfort those who grieve, and heal relationships fractured by hate. Teach us to reflect Your love in every word and action, showing kindness to strangers and care for the vulnerable. Inspire global leaders to*

prioritize compassion and justice, allowing Your kingdom values to shape their decisions. Give us the courage to pursue reconciliation in our lives, modeling Your forgiveness and grace. May every act we take glorify Your name and advance Your work in the world. Amen.

Soul Prayer

Lord Jesus,

Awaken every culture to a longing for Your love. Let nations discover their worth in You, and let communities reflect Your compassion by welcoming strangers and serving the vulnerable. Strengthen Your church to stand boldly as agents of hope, forgiveness, and unity in divided places. May Your truth guide leaders, citizens, and believers alike to seek redemption through Your grace. May Your light shine in dark corners of the world, drawing nations to Your peace and healing. Inspire us to follow Your example, standing firm in faith and love. Amen.

Mind Prayer

Holy Spirit,

Grant us the wisdom to see the world's challenges through Your lens of truth. Teach us to think critically about justice, reconciliation, and equality, responding with integrity and courage. Help leaders govern with discernment, prioritizing the needs of the oppressed and vulnerable. Let every thought align with Your Word and guide our decisions to reflect Your heart. May we see conflict as an opportunity for reconciliation and brokenness as an invitation for Your restoration. Let our minds be anchored in Your promises, creating clarity in the face of complexity. Amen.

Strength Prayer

God Three-in-One,

Empower us to stand firm as Your representatives in a world desperate for Your love. Strengthen us to serve selflessly, advocate boldly for justice, and offer hope to the broken. Remind us that Your power is made perfect in weakness and that every effort made in faith is part of Your plan. Fill us with resilience to face challenges and courage to speak truth in love. Transform our actions into reflections of Your mercy and grace, inspiring others to trust in You. May Your kingdom come and may every step we take honor Your name.

For Thine is the kingdom, Lord Jesus
Thine is the power, Holy Spirit
And Thine is the glory, Heavenly Father,
forever. Amen.

~

The world reflects the Creator's love in its diversity and beauty, yet it longs for restoration. Imagine nations turning to God for guidance, communities fostering peace, and individuals living out His grace. Every act of faith—praying for global leaders, supporting those in need, or standing for justice—contributes to this renewal. Today, let your actions reflect God's heart by showing kindness, lifting a prayer for those suffering, or helping a cause that aligns with His kingdom. Trust that your faithfulness, though small, is part of His greater plan to heal and transform the earth, bringing glimpses of His eternal peace and justice into a waiting world.

NOTES:

DAY 13

Trusting God to Provide for Our Home

Give us this day our daily bread.
(Matthew 6:11, KJV)

The home is a sacred refuge where love, trust, and provision intertwine. Jesus' prayer, Give us this day our daily bread, reminds us of our complete dependence on God's goodness. His provision extends far beyond physical needs, filling our hearts with peace, guiding us through challenges, and strengthening us for the journey ahead. A family's faith, much like bread, sustains them when life feels uncertain. When we trust God, we affirm His care for every detail of our lives. The sparrows that He feeds, the lilies that He clothes—each reflects His promise to meet our needs with love and abundance.

BESIDE QUIET WATERS

One family faced a season of profound financial difficulty after the father lost his job. Gathered around a table with modest meals, they prayed together each night, choosing gratitude over despair. Their prayers invited God's presence into their home, transforming their fear into faith. Friends brought unexpected gifts of groceries. A charity stepped in with assistance, and a neighbor offered encouragement. When the father found a new job, their hearts swelled with gratitude for God's provision, which came through the hands of those around them. Their story became a reminder that God's faithfulness often works through His people.

God longs for our homes to reflect His care—not just for our physical needs but for the deeper hungers of our souls. Jesus, the Bread of Life, satisfies longings that no material possession can fill. His Word nourishes us, bringing peace when we worry and joy when we trust. Imagine a home where fear gives way to thanksgiving, where children grow in faith as they witness answered prayers, and where the family's foundation rests on His promises. May we surrender our anxieties to Him, confident that His provision is both sufficient and abundant. In trusting Him, we discover His perfect care.

The world celebrates independence and self-reliance, urging us to build security in wealth or possessions. God invites us to a radically different posture—one of trust, gratitude, and open-hearted generosity. All we have flows from His hand and sharing what He has provided honors His faithfulness. A widow in Scripture gave all she had, trusting that God would provide for her. This act of sacrificial giving continues to inspire believers to live with open hearts. Let your home reflect this same trust in God's care by becoming a place of generosity, gratitude, and love. His provision is a reminder of His heart for us, calling us to trust Him with all we have.

RIVERS OF LIVING WATER

In His earthly ministry, Jesus demonstrated unwavering trust in God's provision. When thousands gathered with no food, He lifted a prayer of gratitude and broke a meager offering of loaves and fishes. That small meal, placed in God's hands, multiplied to satisfy the crowd and overflowed with abundance. This moment reminds us that no need is too great or too small for God to meet. His power to provide is not limited by what we have but is released through our trust. Prayers rooted in faith invite God's provision into our homes, opening the door for Him to work in extraordinary ways.

The Holy Spirit teaches us to trust God fully in every season. He reminds us of past provision, calming our fears with the assurance of His care. He shapes our hearts to reflect God's generosity, helping us steward what we have for His glory and the good of others. A woman once shared how the Spirit prompted her to deliver a meal to a struggling neighbor. What seemed like a small act of kindness turned into a lifeline for a family in need. God often uses our obedience to reveal His faithfulness, multiplying blessings beyond what we could imagine.

Engage every part of your being—heart, soul, mind, and strength—in seeking God's provision for your home. Build a rhythm of gratitude through prayer, thanking Him for what He has already provided while trusting Him for what lies ahead. Look for ways to reflect His love by meeting the needs of others, whether through encouragement, shared meals, or acts of service. Trusting God deepens our faith, allowing us to rest in His promises and model His care to those around us. Let your home become a testimony of His faithfulness, a place where His provision overflows into acts of generosity and love.

DEEP CALLS TO DEEP

Pause and reflect on the phrase, Give us this day our daily bread. Are there places in your home where worry or fear about provision has taken root? God invites us to release these anxieties into His hands, trusting that His care is constant and His resources limitless. Gratitude becomes the doorway to His peace, helping us focus on His faithfulness instead of our fears. Reflect on the ways He has provided in the past—through a kind word, an unexpected gift, or a timely answer to prayer. Trust that His provision is not only sufficient but abundant, and rest in the assurance of His love.

Heart Prayer

> *Dear Heavenly Father,*
>
> *Fill our hearts with trust in Your faithful provision. Replace our anxieties with peace and confidence in Your care. Help us to see Your hand in every blessing, big or small, and teach us to rest in Your promises. May our homes be places where gratitude flourishes and faith grows. Strengthen us to reflect Your love by sharing Your blessings with others. We*

*trust in Your perfect timing and unfailing
care. Amen.*

Soul Prayer

Lord Jesus,

*Transform our homes into places of
worship and trust. Teach us to rely on You
for every need, drawing strength from
Your Word and hope from Your promises.
Help each member of our family to see You
as the Bread of Life, who satisfies every
longing. May our faith in Your provision
inspire those around us, and may we
always find our peace in Your presence.
Amen.*

Mind Prayer

Holy Spirit,

*Grant us wisdom to manage our resources
with integrity and purpose. Guide our
thoughts to focus on what truly matters
and remind us of God's faithfulness in
every season. Help us to make decisions
that honor Him and reflect our trust in
His care. Fill our minds with gratitude
and teach us to see His provision in every
aspect of our lives. Amen.*

Strength Prayer

> *God Three-in-One,*
>
> *Empower us to face challenges with faith and courage. Strengthen our resolve to trust in Your provision, even when circumstances are difficult. Teach us to be faithful stewards of what You've given us and to share generously with others. May our homes be filled with Your love, peace, and joy, and may they become reflections of Your kingdom.*
>
> *For Thine is the kingdom, Lord Jesus*
> *Thine is the power, Holy Spirit*
> *And Thine is the glory, Heavenly Father,*
> *forever. Amen.*
>
> ~

God's kingdom begins with a heart surrendered to Him, radiating outward into our actions and relationships. Each choice—offering a kind word, forgiving a wrong, or lifting someone in prayer—reflects His love. Imagine a life where His peace shapes your every moment, transforming your home, workplace, and community. Today, take a step toward this transformation by seeking His will in a specific area of your life. Ask Him to guide your thoughts and actions, trusting that even small acts of obedience can ripple into lasting change. As you align your heart with His purpose, you'll see His presence at work, drawing others closer to His love and truth.

DAY 14

Trusting God to Provide for Our Neighborhood

Give us today our daily bread.
(Matthew 6:11, NIV)

Neighborhoods are vibrant reflections of shared humanity, woven with unique needs and opportunities for care. When Jesus teaches us to pray, "Give us today our daily bread," He invites us to trust in God's provision not only for ourselves but also for those around us. This prayer is a reminder that God's love knows no boundaries and that we, as His people, are called to mirror His abundant care. Imagine the joy of being part of a community where God's provision flows freely, uniting hearts in gratitude and compassion.

BESIDE QUIET WATERS

Mrs. Johnson's hands worked the soil with care, her garden yielding baskets of fresh produce that nourished both bodies and souls. She gave generously, her offerings a quiet testimony to God's goodness. Across the street, Mr. Smith mended broken fences with an attentive smile, asking for nothing in return. These acts of kindness weren't grand, but they spoke volumes, planting seeds of hope and connection. Can you picture such a neighborhood, where small gestures ripple outward, creating a mosaic of God's grace? Even the simplest acts of love, done in His name, carry the weight of eternity.

Neighborhoods are sacred spaces where love can thrive, shaped by hearts that reflect God's call to compassion. The Shema reminds us to love God with all our heart, soul, mind, and strength—and to let that love overflow to our neighbors. Imagine a street filled with life-giving relationships, where every interaction whispers His name, and every need met becomes a testimony to His provision. When we embrace His call, our neighborhoods transform into havens of peace, unity, and mutual care, shining brightly with His love.

The world encourages us to seek self-interest, hoard resources, and build walls of separation. Yet, God's kingdom calls us to live differently. Sharing what we have—be it food, time, or skills—creates bridges of understanding and compassion. In serving our neighbors, we hallow God's name, allowing His love to shine through our actions. Pray for eyes to see the needs around you and hands willing to meet them. Through these simple acts of faithfulness, God's provision becomes tangible, and His glory is made known in your neighborhood.

RIVERS OF LIVING WATER

Jesus crossed cultural and societal boundaries to reveal the heart of God. He comforted the lonely, fed the hungry, and reached out to the forgotten, reminding us that His provision knows no limits. His ministry calls us to step beyond our comfort zones, bringing God's love to every corner of our neighborhoods. Pray for the isolated, the struggling, and the spiritually hungry around you. Let your prayers flow like rivers of living water, quenching their deepest thirst with God's provision.

In one neighborhood, a struggling single mother received meals and prayers from a church community. The Holy Spirit used those small acts to transform her despair into hope. He equips us to love others as ourselves, tearing down barriers of fear or prejudice. When we embrace His leading, our communities become vibrant places where God's grace flourishes. Pray for wisdom and courage to respond to your neighbors' needs, trusting Him to guide you. As His love flows through us, His kingdom becomes visible in every interaction.

Devote every aspect of yourself to prayer and service, embracing God's call to live purposefully for His glory. When we offer our time, talents, and resources, God uses them to bring transformation to the lives of others. This heartfelt act of surrender is a profound expression of our trust in His unfailing wisdom and divine plan.

DEEP CALLS TO DEEP

Prayer has the power to transform ordinary spaces into sacred ground. Reflect on the phrase, "Give us today our daily bread." What does it mean to trust God's provision for your neighborhood? Small, faithful acts of kindness—like sharing a meal or mending a fence—can illuminate His presence and turn our streets into shining lights of His love. Trust Him to work through your faithfulness, inspiring ripples of grace.

Heart Prayer

Dear Heavenly Father,

Fill our neighborhoods with Your peace. Replace fear with trust, scarcity with abundance, and separation with unity. Help us see the needs around us and respond with generosity and grace. May Your presence bring comfort to the hurting and peace to every home. Teach us to reflect Your love in every interaction, creating communities that honor Your name. Amen.

Soul Prayer

Lord Jesus,

Open the hearts of our neighbors to Your blessings and let us be instruments of Your love. Cultivate gratitude within us for the ways You provide, even in the smallest moments. Strengthen our faith to trust in Your care and inspire acts of kindness that reveal Your presence. May our neighborhoods flourish as places of connection, support, and faith in You. Amen.

Mind Prayer

Holy Spirit,

Guide our thoughts as we engage with our neighbors. Give us wisdom to manage resources faithfully and compassion to prioritize others above ourselves. May Your Word shape our actions, helping us serve with intentionality and grace. Teach us to see how our small acts, done in faith, can bring transformation. May our neighborhoods reflect Your truth and thrive in Your care. Amen.

Strength Prayer

God Three-in-One,

Equip us to serve with humility and courage. May our hands be extensions of Your love and our words be filled with encouragement. Teach us to live boldly, embodying Your grace in every act of service.

For Thine is the kingdom, Lord Jesus
Thine is the power, Holy Spirit
And Thine is the glory, Heavenly Father,
forever. Amen.

~

God's grace flows into every corner of our lives when we choose trust and surrender. Each moment of faith—whether a whispered prayer, an act of service, or a choice to follow His lead—carries the potential to reflect His transforming power. Picture your life as a vessel, filled with His presence and poured out to bring hope and renewal to others. Today, pause to reflect on His goodness and ask Him to direct your steps. Whether you face challenges or joys, let your actions honor Him. Trust that as you walk in faith, He will use your life to share His love and create ripples of transformation that extend far beyond what you can see.

NOTES:

DAY 15

Trusting God to Provide for Our Community

Give us our food for today.
(Matthew 6:11, CEV)

Communities are tapestries woven with shared moments, unspoken connections, and opportunities to reflect God's love. Jesus' words, "Give us our food for today," remind us that God's provision extends beyond our individual needs to encompass the collective needs of the places we call home. Each interaction is a chance to reveal His abundant care, as our trust in Him transforms ordinary connections into reflections of His kingdom.

BESIDE QUIET WATERS

A city once divided by economic challenges began to heal when local churches united to create a community kitchen. Imagine the aroma of warm bread, the hum of shared laughter, and the gentle murmur of prayers filling the room. These moments fostered relationships across cultural and generational lines, replacing division with connection. Volunteers served meals with tender compassion, embodying God's provision in action. One young mother, hesitant at first, found hope in a warm meal and a kind word, reminding her of God's faithfulness. Such simple acts of care become breadcrumbs of grace, leading others to the abundance of His love.

God envisions communities as sanctuaries of His kingdom, where love, compassion, and gratitude overflow into every interaction. The Shema's call to love God with all our heart, soul, mind, and strength is a directive to extend that love into our neighborhoods and cities. Picture businesses rooted in integrity, schools nurturing both knowledge and kindness, and streets alive with connection. These visions become reality when we trust in God's provision and respond by sharing His blessings with others. How might you, today, become a reflection of His care in your community?

The world urges us to focus on self-interest and accumulation, but God invites us to live differently. His kingdom calls us to generosity and empathy, where the act of sharing transforms lives. A single meal, a kind word, or a listening ear can bridge divides, creating bonds of trust and unity. Pray for eyes to recognize the needs around you and hands willing to respond. Through simple yet faithful acts, God's provision flows outward, strengthening relationships and glorifying His name. What role will you play in the transformation of your community?

RIVERS OF LIVING WATER

Jesus modeled God's heart for provision through acts of compassion and restoration. Whether feeding multitudes with a few loaves and fish or reaching out to the forgotten, His actions demonstrated the boundless nature of God's care. He invites us to follow His example by engaging with the challenges in our communities through prayer and tangible service. Small steps of faith, guided by prayer, create streams of provision that flow into places of need, bringing renewal and hope.

In one small town, neighbors gathered in prayer, asking for God's guidance in addressing a growing need for educational support. Their prayers inspired a tutoring program at a local church, where volunteers offered time and resources to struggling students. A young boy, once on the verge of giving up, began to thrive academically and emotionally under their care. His laughter and newfound confidence became a testament to the power of collective prayer and action. The Holy Spirit equips us to love others deeply, breaking down barriers of fear and prejudice, and creating communities that flourish with grace.

Engage every part of yourself in prayer and service. Lift up leaders, families, and educators in your community, asking God to bless their efforts and provide for their needs. Consider ways you can contribute—through mentoring, supporting local initiatives, or fostering moments of connection and care. Together, our prayers and actions reflect the rivers of God's provision, turning communities into places where His love is both seen and felt.

DEEP CALLS TO DEEP

Prayer invites God's presence into the heart of our communities, transforming them into sacred spaces. The phrase, "Give us our food for today," is a reminder that God's provision flows through acts of faith and love.

Imagine a community where small gestures of kindness, like a shared meal or a word of encouragement, reveal His presence and inspire hope. Trust that your prayers and actions, rooted in faith, will ripple outward to touch lives and glorify His name.

Heart Prayer

Dear Heavenly Father,

Fill our communities with Your peace. Replace fear with trust, division with unity, and scarcity with abundance. Help us to see and respond to the needs around us with open hearts and willing hands. May Your presence bring comfort to the weary, hope to the discouraged, and strength to the struggling. Teach us to reflect Your love in every action, creating communities that honor Your name and reveal Your provision. Amen.

Soul Prayer

Lord Jesus,

Open the hearts of our neighbors to recognize Your blessings in their lives. Cultivate gratitude in us for Your abundant care and strengthen our faith to trust in Your provision. Inspire acts of kindness that mirror Your love, turning ordinary streets into places of connection and support. May our neighborhoods thrive as spaces of faith, hope, and love, reflecting Your kingdom to all who enter. Amen.

Mind Prayer

Holy Spirit,

Guide our thoughts as we discern how to meet the needs of our communities. Grant us wisdom to steward resources faithfully and compassion to prioritize others above ourselves. Shape our actions with Your truth and lead us to serve with intentionality and grace. May our efforts reflect Your love and bring about transformation in the lives of those we touch. Amen.

Strength Prayer

God Three-in-One,

Empower us to serve boldly, with courage and humility. Let our hands extend Your care through every act of service, and our words bring encouragement to those in need. Equip us to live as ambassadors of Your kingdom, embodying Your grace in all we do

For Thine is the kingdom, Lord Jesus
Thine is the power, Holy Spirit
And Thine is the glory, Heavenly Father,
forever. Amen.

~

God's faithfulness transforms even the smallest steps of trust into lasting impact. Each time you lean on Him, your obedience becomes a channel for His hope to reach others in unseen ways. Picture a life marked by peace, where acts of kindness and moments of prayer radiate His love. Today, choose to place your challenges in His hands and let His Spirit guide your actions. Whether you speak a word of encouragement, offer forgiveness, or extend a helping hand, trust that He is working through you. Step forward with confidence, knowing that your faith is part of His unfolding plan to draw hearts closer to His kingdom.

NOTES:

DAY 16

Trusting God to Provide for Our State

Give us this day our daily bread.
(Matthew 6:11, ESV)

The beauty of our state, from its sweeping farmland to the bustling streets of its cities, reflects God's hand of provision. Each field of grain, each thriving business, and each quiet community whispers His care and creativity. When Jesus prayed, "Give us this day our daily bread," He invited us to recognize God as the source of all provision—not just for individuals but for entire communities and systems. Trusting Him daily opens our eyes to His blessings, deepens our gratitude, and inspires us to share His love and resources with others.

BESIDE QUIET WATERS

In the aftermath of a devastating storm, an entire county rallied in resilience. Volunteers distributed meals, cleared debris, and rebuilt homes. Among them was a local pastor who said, "When everything seems lost, God's love comes alive in the hands of His people." Children played amidst the rubble, their laughter a song of hope, while neighbors offered each other comfort and care. These acts of service were seeds of healing, showing how God's provision flows through unity and compassion. What role might you play in bringing hope and renewal to the places around you?

The early church offers a timeless example of this collective care. As Acts 2:44-45 tells us, believers shared what they had, ensuring no one went without. Imagine our state shaped by this same spirit of generosity: leaders choosing integrity over ambition, neighborhoods fostering kindness, and communities thriving on trust and shared purpose. God's kingdom shines brightest when His people respond in love to His abundant provision. How can your life reflect His care for others today?

The world often celebrates power, independence, and wealth, urging us to focus on self-interest. Yet God calls us to humility and service, using what we have to bless others. Mentoring a young leader, supporting an ethical business, or praying for state officials are simple but profound ways to reflect His heart. Trust Him to magnify these small acts of faith, creating ripples of transformation that extend far beyond what we can see. How might your community change if every person trusted in God's provision and shared it freely?

RIVERS OF LIVING WATER

Jesus' ministry consistently revealed the transformative power of provision. He healed the sick, fed the hungry, and restored dignity to the forgotten, showing us that God's love meets both physical and spiritual needs. When we intercede for our state, we join in this mission, aligning our hearts with His purposes. Prayer is like rain on thirsty ground, nourishing dry places and bringing forth life. Imagine the impact when prayers for schools, healthcare workers, and leaders ripple through our communities, touching hearts and inspiring change.

In one state, prayer for systemic reform led to a surprising breakthrough. Believers prayed for struggling students, and soon, a community-driven tutoring program was born. A discouraged teenager found hope in the care of a mentor who helped her see God's provision in her life. These small steps of obedience, guided by prayer, create environments where grace flourishes. Trust the Holy Spirit to guide you in prayer and action, knowing He equips you to bring renewal to the spaces He has called you to serve.

Take a tangible step by writing a letter of encouragement to a state leader, thanking them for their service and reminding them of the prayers being lifted for them. As we combine prayer with tangible expressions of love, we reflect God's provision in ways that can't be ignored. Engage with your whole heart, soul, mind, and strength. Pray fervently for teachers, healthcare providers, and local businesses. Volunteer to support a struggling school, advocate for equitable policies, or lend a hand at a food bank. These actions create a testimony of faith in action, demonstrating the kingdom of God in practical ways.

DEEP CALLS TO DEEP

"Give us this day our daily bread" is not just a personal request but a collective cry for God's provision across our state. Reflect on the needs around you—broken systems, struggling families, and overlooked communities—and ask how you can be a part of His solution. Even small, faithful steps become avenues for His grace to flow, inspiring transformation and healing.

Heart Prayer

Dear Heavenly Father,

Fill our state with Your peace. Where division lingers, plant unity. Where despair thrives, grow hope. Strengthen weary hands and uplift burdened hearts. Inspire our leaders to act with justice and wisdom, reflecting Your character in every decision. May Your presence bring renewal to our communities, making them sanctuaries of Your grace. Teach us to trust in Your abundant provision and to share it with open hearts. Amen.

Soul Prayer

Lord Jesus,

Awaken the hearts of our state's people to Your love. Help our leaders govern with humility and courage, and let citizens reflect Your kindness in their interactions. Replace conflict with reconciliation and fear with faith. Show us how to embrace Your will and trust in Your care. May our state become a reflection of Your kingdom,

*where compassion triumphs over division
and hope springs eternal. Amen.*

Mind Prayer

Holy Spirit,

*Guide us with Your wisdom as we face the
challenges in our state. Illuminate the
paths that lead to justice, equity, and
peace. Help us to see opportunities to serve
and meet needs with creativity and grace.
May Your Word shape our decisions,
ensuring they reflect Your truth. May our
thoughts be anchored in Your promises,
leading to actions that transform lives and
glorify Your name. Amen.*

Strength Prayer

God Three-in-One,

*Equip us to persevere in love and service.
Strengthen us to act boldly, trusting in
Your provision as we care for our
communities. Let our words and actions be
instruments of Your grace, creating ripples
of hope and restoration. May our efforts
glorify You and inspire others to seek Your
heart.*

For Thine is the kingdom, Lord Jesus

*Thine is the power, Holy Spirit
And Thine is the glory, Heavenly Father,
forever. Amen.*

~

A home filled with God's presence becomes a sanctuary of love and restoration. Every shared prayer, every word of encouragement, and every moment of grace creates an atmosphere where His Spirit works. Imagine your household as a place where patience replaces frustration, joy rises above challenges, and faith anchors each day. Today, invite God into your daily rhythms. Whether it's a prayer before a meal, a quiet act of kindness, or a conversation that fosters understanding, trust that He is transforming your home into a reflection of His kingdom. As you take these steps, His peace will deepen your relationships and renew the heart of your home.

NOTES:

DAY 17

Trusting God to Provide for Our Nation

Give us today our daily bread.
(Matthew 6:11, HCSB)

Prayer is not just asking but aligning with God's purposes, as Jesus demonstrated when He sought the Father's will before every major decision. The Civil Rights Movement, steeped in prayer, showcased how reliance on God's guidance united communities and restored hope. Similarly, when we pray for our leaders and neighbors, we invite Him to bring healing and renewal that echoes His kingdom's justice and peace.

BESIDE QUIET WATERS

During the Civil Rights Movement, leaders like Dr. Martin Luther King Jr. sought God's wisdom through fervent prayer. Marches and peaceful protests were steeped in faith, their steps guided by the belief that justice aligns with God's heart. These acts of trust in God's provision brought about systemic changes that began to heal a divided nation. Such moments of history remind us that when a nation seeks God, His hand moves mightily, providing wisdom and strength to overcome even the most entrenched challenges. Imagine leaders today pursuing integrity, businesses committed to fairness, and communities embodying God's compassion. What might God do through a nation that fully depends on Him?

God's vision for a nation includes justice, mercy, and compassion. As the Shema calls us to love Him with all our heart, soul, mind, and strength, that love must overflow into our civic life. Picture a nation where laws reflect righteousness, leaders govern with humility, and citizens care deeply for one another. Trusting God's provision unites us in purpose, creating communities where every need—physical, emotional, and spiritual—is met through His abundance. Our faith in His care inspires advocacy for the vulnerable and empowers us to bring His kingdom values to life.

The systems of the world frequently prioritize power and self-interest, often neglecting the needs of the vulnerable. God calls us to a different way, one marked by humility and sacrificial service to others. By following His example, we can become reflections of His love, bringing transformation and hope into every area of our influence.

RIVERS OF LIVING WATER

Jesus often withdrew to pray, seeking alignment with the Father's will. His life shows us that prayer is not simply asking but becoming attuned to God's purposes. When Jesus taught His disciples to pray for "daily bread," He emphasized reliance on God's provision for every need.

In the context of a nation, prayer becomes a powerful tool for renewal and unity. Through prayer, we invite God to guide our leaders, heal our communities, and restore what is broken.

After September 11, 2001, churches and public spaces filled with people crying out to God for peace and direction. This collective prayer reflected a nation's dependence on Him during a time of grief. Out of this sorrow, acts of kindness and unity flourished—neighbors helping neighbors, strangers becoming friends. These moments revealed how prayer not only strengthens faith but transforms hearts, creating a ripple effect of compassion and resilience. Trust the Holy Spirit to guide your prayers, knowing He intercedes when words fail, aligning your heart with God's purposes for our nation.

Advocacy paired with prayer reflects the heart of God's kingdom. Writing a letter of encouragement to a state leader, mentoring a young person, or volunteering at a local shelter are tangible ways to embody His love. Imagine the impact when believers unite in prayer and action, creating waves of hope and restoration across a nation. As we align ourselves with God's purposes, even small acts become significant, reflecting His provision and care for the people and systems around us.

DEEP CALLS TO DEEP

"Give us today our daily bread" is a prayer of trust and dependence. It invites us to lean on God's provision not just for our personal needs but for the challenges our nation faces. By trusting Him, we become part of His work, reflecting His peace and provision through both prayer and action.

Heart Prayer

Dear Heavenly Father,

Fill our nation with Your peace. Replace division with unity, despair with hope, and conflict with reconciliation. Comfort those who mourn and strengthen leaders to act with wisdom and integrity. Teach us to trust Your provision for every need, knowing Your faithfulness never falters. May Your love inspire us to serve others, building a nation where Your presence is felt in every home and community. Amen.

Soul Prayer

Lord Jesus,

Awaken the hearts of leaders and citizens to seek You first. May Your peace replace fear, and Your truth replace confusion. Inspire us to see one another as Your creation, working together for justice and compassion. Transform relationships marked by conflict into ones rooted in grace. May our nation reflect the values of Your kingdom, becoming a shining light of hope and love to the world. Amen.

Mind Prayer

Holy Spirit,

Guide the minds of our leaders as they navigate complex decisions. Grant wisdom, discernment, and clarity, shaping policies that reflect Your justice and mercy. Help citizens to think deeply and act wisely, responding to challenges with grace and understanding. May Your Word shape the thoughts of every person in positions of influence, bringing about unity and purpose that honors You. Amen.

Strength Prayer

God Three-in-One,

Equip us to persevere in love and service. Strengthen us to reflect Your character in every act of kindness, generosity, and courage. Empower leaders to lead with integrity and inspire citizens to work together for the common good. Let every action glorify Your name, bringing transformation and renewal to our nation.

For Thine is the kingdom, Lord Jesus
Thine is the power, Holy Spirit
And Thine is the glory, Heavenly Father,
forever. Amen.

~

God's love transforms even the simplest moments into opportunities for His grace to shine. When we align our hearts with His purpose, the ordinary becomes sacred, and small choices reflect His presence. Imagine your life as a steady light, guiding others toward hope and peace through acts of kindness and words of encouragement. Today, ask God to strengthen your faith and lead your steps, trusting that every decision made in obedience to Him creates a ripple of His love. As you walk in His grace, watch how He uses your faithfulness to bring comfort and renewal to the lives you touch.

DAY 18

Trusting God to Provide for Our World

Give us this day our daily bread.
(Matthew 6:11, NASB)

The world is a mosaic of vibrant beauty and aching brokenness, a reflection of both creation's glory and humanity's deep need. Jesus' words, "Give us this day our daily bread," are a lifeline, reminding us of our dependence on God's abundant provision. Every sunrise, every drop of rain, and every meal on our tables bear witness to His faithfulness. When we trust Him to meet our needs, gratitude grows, and faith flourishes. His provision is steadfast, caring for both the sparrow and His beloved children.

BESIDE QUIET WATERS

Amina, a young girl from an arid village, once carried the weight of survival on her small shoulders. Her days revolved around arduous treks to fetch water for her family. Everything changed when a local organization installed a well in her community. The well transformed their lives—children laughed as water splashed from buckets, and Amina's smile shone brighter as she walked to school instead of the distant river. Her story of renewal mirrors the power of God's provision, reminding us to trust Him and to reflect His care through our actions.

God's vision for the world is one of restoration, justice, and flourishing. The Shema calls us to love Him with our whole being—heart, soul, mind, and strength. This love, when truly embraced, spills over into action. Like Elijah trusting God's provision by the brook Cherith, we too can rest in His faithfulness. His resources are sufficient to meet the world's needs, and His call to us is to become participants in His kingdom's work. Each step we take to love and serve others reflects His heart and advances His purposes.

In a world captivated by self-interest, God invites us to walk a path marked by humility, mercy, and justice. Prayerful action—whether advocating for fair resource distribution, supporting global aid, or simply choosing compassion in daily decisions—illuminates His kingdom values. These small acts, fueled by faith, carry the weight of eternity, touching lives with His grace. Every choice to love and serve becomes a testimony to His provision and a shining light of hope in the darkness.

RIVERS OF LIVING WATER

Jesus demonstrated complete trust in God's provision. When feeding the five thousand, He began with gratitude, lifting His eyes to heaven and giving thanks. What seemed insufficient became more than enough, multiplying in God's hands. This profound example calls us to face global challenges with unwavering faith, knowing prayer connects us to the source of all provision. Through prayer, we partner with God in bringing His abundance into a world in need.

Following a devastating hurricane, a small rural church became a refuge for its community, offering food, shelter, and the reassurance of hope. Church members devoted themselves to rebuilding homes and restoring lives, embodying the selfless love of Christ. Through their tireless efforts, they demonstrated what it means to serve as the hands and feet of Jesus in times of great need.

Prayer serves as the starting point for meaningful action. By trusting in God's guidance, we are empowered to take steps that align our efforts with His divine will. This partnership with God not only fuels our actions but also ensures a lasting and transformative impact in the world.

DEEP CALLS TO DEEP

Meditate on the prayer, "Give us this day our daily bread," and consider the global needs pressing on your heart. How might your faith translate into action? Each step, however small, contributes to a world touched by His love and justice. Trust that God is already at work and let your actions flow from confidence in His unwavering provision.

Heart Prayer

Dear Heavenly Father,

Fill the world with the peace that only You can provide. Transform the conflicts that divide us into bridges of understanding and turn hatred into expressions of love. Empower us to be instruments of Your divine harmony, bringing unity and healing wherever it is needed.

Soul Prayer

Lord Jesus,

Awaken hearts across the world to Your truth. Lead nations to embrace Your values, shaping their actions to reflect Your kingdom. Unite diverse cultures in love and respect, building communities that glorify You. Transform societies through Your grace, allowing faith to flourish and righteousness to thrive. May Your name be praised in every corner of the earth. Amen.

Mind Prayer

Holy Spirit,

Grant us wisdom to face the complexities of global challenges. Shape our thoughts to reflect Your truth and guide our actions toward mercy and justice. Help us prioritize the needs of others, reflecting Your love in all we do. Fill us with a vision of hope and peace as we work for a better world. Amen.

Strength Prayer

God Three-in-One,

Empower us to serve with courage and perseverance. Strengthen our resolve to meet challenges with grace, offering solutions inspired by Your love. Use us to build communities that reflect Your kingdom. Let every act of service bring You glory and draw others to Your presence.

For Thine is the kingdom, Lord Jesus
Thine is the power, Holy Spirit
And Thine is the glory, Heavenly Father,
forever. Amen.

~

God meets us in the quiet decisions of daily life, inviting us to share His peace with those we encounter. Each choice to extend kindness, offer a prayer, or encourage a weary heart reflects His love. Today, ask Him to guide you toward someone in need of His presence. Trust that even your smallest acts of faith will carry His light into the world.

NOTES:

DAY 19

Restoring Relationships in Our Home

And forgive us our debts, as we forgive our debtors. (Matthew 6:12, KJV)

The home is a sanctuary, where love is nurtured, and wounds can heal. Yet, it is also the space where our flaws are most visible. Jesus' words, "And forgive us our debts, as we forgive our debtors," invite us to embrace forgiveness as a daily practice. By doing so, we allow God's grace to dissolve bitterness and renew relationships. Forgiveness is the cornerstone of building a home filled with trust, joy, and peace.

BESIDE QUIET WATERS

A family gathered for a holiday dinner, the table adorned with heirloom dishes and fragrant with roasted turkey. Beneath the laughter, a quiet tension lingered—old wounds, long buried, threatened to surface. A brave voice broke through the discomfort. "I've been holding onto resentment, and I need to ask for forgiveness." Tears welled, walls crumbled, and a hug sealed the moment. Bitterness gave way to grace, reminding all present of the power of vulnerability and the healing that follows.

God longs for our homes to reflect His love and mercy. The Shema calls us to love Him with all our heart, soul, mind, and strength, and that love overflows into our relationships. Forgiveness becomes a tangible act of that love, healing broken bonds and creating a sanctuary of grace. Imagine a home where apology and reconciliation are met with open arms—a haven where God's presence transforms each relationship. This vision is not beyond reach; it is God's invitation to every family.

The world promotes holding onto offenses, but God calls us to something higher. By choosing forgiveness, we allow His love to shine through us, turning moments of conflict into opportunities for grace. A simple apology or an intentional act of reconciliation can spark a ripple effect of healing. Homes anchored in forgiveness become reflections of His kingdom, where grace reigns and His name is glorified.

RIVERS OF LIVING WATER

Jesus vividly modeled forgiveness through both His teachings and His actions. On the cross, He extended grace to those who wronged Him, embodying the depth of God's mercy. His extraordinary example challenges us to embrace forgiveness, regardless of the personal cost, as a reflection of His boundless love.

A young couple, burdened by years of misunderstandings, reached a breaking point. Through prayer, they asked the Holy Spirit to guide them. "Let's begin again," the husband said, his voice trembling. In the quietness of their living room, they prayed together, inviting God into their pain. The Spirit softened their hearts, replacing resentment with compassion and renewing their love. This is the transformative power of forgiveness when we are guided by the Spirit.

Forgiveness requires intention and a willingness to trust God's strength. In moments of tension, praying for wisdom and humility allows His Spirit to lead us toward reconciliation. Each act of forgiveness we extend brings us closer to the heart of Christ, who forgave us even in His suffering. Imagine a home where forgiveness is not rare but regular, a rhythm that restores harmony and draws others to God's love.

DEEP CALLS TO DEEP

Forgiveness is a bold step of faith, a gift that transforms both the giver and receiver. Reflect on Jesus' prayer, "And forgive us our debts, as we forgive our debtors." What relationships in your home need healing? Trust God to guide you as you pursue reconciliation and invite His grace to bring renewal.

Heart Prayer

> *Dear Heavenly Father,*
>
> *Fill our homes with Your peace. Heal wounds caused by words and actions and teach us to forgive as You have forgiven us.*

*Let our relationships reflect Your mercy,
and may our homes become places where
love flourishes and grace abound.
Transform our hearts with Your presence,
making forgiveness the foundation of our
family's strength. Amen.*

Soul Prayer

Lord Jesus,

*Help us recognize our need for forgiveness
and teach us to extend it freely. Break
down barriers of pride and open our
hearts to reconciliation. May our homes
reflect Your love, becoming sanctuaries of
compassion and joy. Inspire us to model
Your grace in every interaction, so Your
light shines through us. Amen.*

Mind Prayer

Holy Spirit,

*Grant us wisdom in moments of conflict.
Help us choose words that heal instead of
harm and guide us toward resolutions that
honor You. Shape our thoughts to align
with Your truth, reflecting Your peace in
our relationships. May Your wisdom lead
us to forgive boldly and live humbly,
trusting in Your power. Amen.*

Strength Prayer

God Three-in-One,

Strengthen us to forgive with courage, rebuilding trust and restoring love. Help us act with grace even when it feels difficult. Empower us to reflect Your love in every action, transforming our homes into reflections of Your kingdom.

For Thine is the kingdom, Lord Jesus
Thine is the power, Holy Spirit
And Thine is the glory, Heavenly Father,
forever. Amen.

~

God's love transforms every moment we surrender to Him, turning even the ordinary into opportunities to reflect His glory. Each prayer you lift, each act of compassion you offer, becomes part of His work to bring hope and renewal to others. Picture your life as a reflection of His grace, where your words uplift, your actions inspire, and your faith draws others closer to Him. Today, ask God to open your eyes to the opportunities around you to share His love. Trust that He will use your faithfulness to touch lives, planting seeds of peace and joy that will grow in ways you may never imagine.

DAY 20

Restoring Relationships in Our Neighborhood

And forgive us our debts, as we also
have forgiven our debtors.
(Matthew 6:12, NIV)

Neighborhoods are vibrant canvases where lives intersect, blending moments of joy with inevitable conflicts. Jesus' words, "And forgive us our debts, as we also have forgiven our debtors," remind us that forgiveness is a bridge to reconciliation and harmony. When we release grudges and seek understanding, we create a community that mirrors God's grace. Forgiveness fosters not only personal peace but also the collective flourishing of our neighborhoods.

BESIDE QUIET WATERS

Mrs. Harris and Mr. Lee hadn't exchanged more than polite nods for years. A misunderstanding over property boundaries had festered into silence. On an early spring morning, Mrs. Harris walked to Mr. Lee's garden, holding a plate of cookies. Her voice trembled as she said, "I'm sorry for letting this go on so long." Mr. Lee hesitated, then replied, "I've missed having you as a friend." They shared a quiet laugh about old times. Soon, neighbors noticed the change—shared greetings turned into conversations, and once-distant relationships blossomed. This act of courage became a turning point, rippling through the neighborhood and inspiring others to mend their own fractured connections.

God's vision for neighborhoods is that they mirror His kingdom, places where love, peace, and justice thrive. When neighbors extend care and compassion to one another, they amplify His presence in tangible ways. Such expressions of kindness serve as a living testimony to the heart of God, drawing others closer to His transformative love.

The world often encourages grudges and retaliation, but God calls us to a higher standard. Choosing forgiveness, even when it feels difficult, reflects His love and draws His presence into our lives. Approaching a neighbor with an apology or letting go of resentment opens the door for His grace to transform hearts. Picture streets where laughter replaces tension and conversations flow freely. Forgiveness is not just an individual act but a collective step toward creating communities that reflect His kingdom.

RIVERS OF LIVING WATER

Jesus illustrated forgiveness as a pursuit of restoration and unity. In parables like the prodigal son, He shows that forgiveness is not an obligation but a gift of grace that mirrors the Father's heart. When we extend this grace in our neighborhoods, we participate in His redemptive work, fostering connections that reflect His kingdom.

A neglected park had become a symbol of division among neighbors, with heated debates over its maintenance. Then, a child's innocent suggestion—"Why don't we all clean it up together?"—sparked a wave of cooperation. Adults who had barely spoken began working side by side, sharing tools and laughter. By the end of the day, the park was restored, and so were relationships. The Holy Spirit uses these moments to break down barriers, inspiring us to forgive and heal. When we surrender our frustrations to Him, He equips us to rebuild trust and unity in our neighborhoods.

Forgiveness is both a choice and a process, one that requires humility and courage. Praying for guidance softens our hearts and gives us the strength to approach conflicts with grace. Imagine a community where forgiveness flows freely, paving the way for healing and connection. These small acts, guided by prayer and compassion, create neighborhoods where God's presence is felt in every interaction.

DEEP CALLS TO DEEP

Forgiveness requires courage, but it carries the power to transform lives and neighborhoods. Reflect on Jesus' prayer, "And forgive us our debts, as we also have forgiven our debtors." Are there relationships in your neighborhood that need healing? Trust God to guide you as you take steps toward reconciliation, knowing that His grace flows through every act of forgiveness.

Heart Prayer

Dear Heavenly Father,

*Fill our neighborhoods with Your peace.
Heal divisions, soften hardened hearts,
and teach us to forgive as You have
forgiven us. Let our relationships reflect
Your love and grace, creating communities
where trust and kindness thrive. Inspire us
to be vessels of Your reconciliation,
building bridges where walls once stood.
Amen.*

Soul Prayer

Lord Jesus,

*Open our hearts to Your example of
forgiveness. Teach us to love our neighbors
as You love us, extending grace even when
it is undeserved. Transform our
neighborhoods into sanctuaries of peace,
where unity and compassion prevail. May
we walk in Your footsteps, modeling Your
mercy in every interaction. Amen.*

Mind Prayer

Holy Spirit,

*Grant us wisdom to navigate conflicts
with grace and humility. Shape our
thoughts to align with Your truth and
teach us to speak words that heal. Guide us
to see others as You see them, with*

compassion and understanding. May Your presence lead us toward reconciliation, creating communities that honor You. Amen.

Strength Prayer

God Three-in-One,

Empower us to forgive with courage and humility. Strengthen us to rebuild trust where it has been broken and to serve others with Your love. May our actions reflect Your kingdom, transforming our neighborhoods into reflections of Your grace.

For Thine is the kingdom, Lord Jesus
Thine is the power, Holy Spirit
And Thine is the glory, Heavenly Father,
forever. Amen.

~

When we trust God in the small moments, He multiplies their impact for His glory. Each step of obedience—whether through encouragement, forgiveness, or love—shines His light into the lives of others. Today, ask Him to guide your actions and use them for His purposes. Trust that your faith will inspire transformation, bringing His peace and joy to those around you.

NOTES:

DAY 21

Restoring Relationships in Our Community

Forgive us for doing wrong, as we
forgive others.
(Matthew 6:12, CEV)

Communities flourish when relationships are rooted in trust, yet fractures often emerge through misunderstandings or offenses. The words of the Lord's Prayer, "Forgive us for doing wrong, as we forgive others," beckon us to heal what has been broken. Forgiveness is more than a moral obligation; it is God's invitation to extend grace and allow healing to take place. Holding onto anger is like grasping a thorn—it only harms us the longer we cling to it. But forgiveness clears the foggy windshield of our hearts, letting us see the road of reconciliation ahead. By releasing resentment, God's love flows through us, rebuilding broken connections and fostering belonging.

BESIDE QUIET WATERS

Communities often grapple with the burdens of division and conflict. True healing begins when we choose to listen with open hearts and extend grace to one another. In the act of reconciliation, we not only mend relationships but also reflect the unity and harmony of God's kingdom, fostering peace and understanding.

God envisions communities as places of restoration, where forgiveness flourishes like a gentle rain, washing away bitterness and breathing new life into relationships. As we love God with all our heart, soul, mind, and strength, His love naturally overflows into our interactions with others. When communities reflect God's kingdom, compassion and reconciliation become the norm. Forgiveness aligns us with His plan, bringing His light into our lives and the lives of those around us. By forgiving others, we choose trust over suspicion and unity over division, becoming instruments of grace that ripple outward into the world.

While the world often glorifies vengeance and nurtures grudges, God calls us to follow a higher and more freeing path. Forgiveness lifts the heavy burden of anger from our hearts and restores fractured relationships. By choosing to forgive, we reflect the heart of Christ, fostering healing and reconciliation for everyone involved.

RIVERS OF LIVING WATER

Jesus demonstrated the restorative power of forgiveness through His life and death. As He hung on the cross, His words, "Father, forgive them, for they know not what they do," pierced through unimaginable pain and injustice. This profound act of grace teaches us that no offense is too great to forgive. Forgiveness, as modeled by Jesus, sets us free from the chains of bitterness and invites reconciliation. Communities transformed by Christ's love are marked by peace and renewal. Choosing forgiveness is like breaking a chain, one link at a time, until we stand liberated by God's grace.

The Holy Spirit equips us with the courage to forgive when our hearts resist. He softens hardened hearts, replacing resentment with compassion and helping us view others through God's eyes. As we surrender past hurts, the Spirit reminds us of the grace we have received and calls us to extend it to others. Just as rain refreshes dry ground, the Spirit heals our wounds and nourishes unity in our communities. Trusting in His power allows us to participate in God's redemptive work, bringing peace and restoration where division once ruled.

Forgiveness demands intentional effort and commitment to God's calling. Engaging our hearts, souls, minds, and strength, we can create rhythms of reconciliation. Begin with prayer, asking God to reveal areas of unforgiveness in your heart. Then take practical steps, such as writing a letter of apology, performing an act of service, or showing unexpected kindness to rebuild trust. Each step reflects Christ's love and creates ripples of transformation, like stones skipped across water. In forgiving, we shine as shining lights of hope, building stronger relationships and fostering a deeper sense of belonging within our communities.

DEEP CALLS TO DEEP

The words, "Forgive us for doing wrong, as we forgive others," challenge us to live in obedience and love. Strained relationships can often leave behind scars of resentment, but God calls us to the courageous act of releasing bitterness. Consider how God's forgiveness has transformed your own life. Extending that forgiveness to others allows His grace to work through you. Reconciliation requires humility and trust, yet it is through this obedience that God's peace flows into our hearts and our communities. Trust in His Spirit to guide and empower you to pursue healing and restoration in every interaction.

Heart Prayer

Dear Heavenly Father,

May Your peace flood our communities, washing away bitterness and resentment. Replace hostility with compassion and help us see the beauty of forgiveness in restoring relationships. Bring healing to those carrying the weight of past hurts, guiding them toward reconciliation. May Your love transform every corner of our community into a haven of grace. Teach us to forgive freely, as You have forgiven us. Make our hearts vessels of Your peace and love, open and ready to serve. Amen.

Soul Prayer

Lord Jesus,

Reveal to us the depth of Your forgiveness through the cross. Teach us to release

*grudges and extend grace to those who
have wronged us, even when it feels
beyond our strength. Strengthen
relationships in our community, making
them reflections of Your kingdom.
Transform our hearts with compassion
and lead us toward reconciliation. Let
grace and unity be the hallmarks of our
communities, bringing hope and healing
wherever we go. May we live in the light
of Your forgiveness, demonstrating it in
every action. Amen.*

Mind Prayer

Holy Spirit,

*Grant us wisdom to navigate conflicts
with clarity and grace. Shape our thoughts
with Your Word, teaching us to approach
challenges with humility and
understanding. Open our eyes to the needs
of others and make us agents of healing in
our communities. Replace judgment with
compassion and anger with empathy. Let
every decision reflect Your truth and use us
to promote peace and unity. May Your
wisdom guide our actions, ensuring that
all we do points others toward
reconciliation and Your love. Amen.*

Strength Prayer

God Three-in-One,

Fill us with strength to forgive those who have wronged us. Grant us the courage to break down walls of bitterness and extend grace. Empower us to rebuild trust through tangible acts of kindness and service. Let forgiveness ripple through our communities, fostering healing and unity. Use our strength to reflect Your heart, inspire reconciliation, and bring peace to every interaction. May we glorify You as we forgive, just as we have been forgiven.

For Thine is the kingdom, Lord Jesus
Thine is the power, Holy Spirit
And Thine is the glory, Heavenly Father,
forever. Amen.

~

Faith becomes a journey of unexpected opportunities when we trust God's hand in every moment. Instead of seeking perfection, focus on taking one deliberate step at a time—whether offering a helping hand, sharing a word of comfort, or standing firm in your convictions. Each of these actions becomes part of His greater story, far beyond what we can foresee. Let today be a time of alignment with His purposes, where your obedience transforms into a reflection of His enduring love. As you walk forward in faith, believe that the seeds you plant now will grow into something only God's grace can sustain. Trust in His plans and watch as His presence shapes the lives you encounter.

DAY 22

Restoring Relationships in Our State

*And forgive us our debts, as we also
have forgiven our debtors.
(Matthew 6:12, ESV)*

The rolling hills, busy urban streets, and expansive farmlands across our nation speak to the magnificent artistry of God. In every corner, from the vibrant markets to the serene sanctuaries, His presence is deeply interwoven into the landscape. As recipients of His blessings, we are called to steward this divine gift with care, reflecting gratitude through our actions and choices.

BESIDE QUIET WATERS

A small rural town divided by a years-long land dispute offers a powerful testimony of reconciliation. Bitterness had seeped into every corner of the community, even dividing a local church. A pastor, burdened by the division, began a series of sermons on forgiveness, encouraging his congregation to mend fences—both literally and figuratively. The first apology was hesitant, but it sparked a flood of conversations and acts of reconciliation. As hammers rang out in the fields, fences were rebuilt, not as barriers, but as shared symbols of unity and hope. The pastor's faithfulness turned the community into a living parable of God's redemptive power.

God's vision for our state reflects His heart for reconciliation. Forgiveness isn't merely a private decision; it overflows into every relationship and institution, transforming them into shining lights of His grace. As the Shema commands, we are called to love God with all our heart, soul, mind, and strength, allowing forgiveness to flow outward. Imagine citizens embracing compassion instead of conflict, policies shaped by restoration rather than retaliation, and leaders guided by humility and wisdom. A state marked by forgiveness reflects God's kingdom—a place where grace restores what is broken, strengthens trust, and ushers in peace.

Society often celebrates holding grudges and seeking revenge, but forgiveness disrupts these cycles, paving the way for healing. Forgiveness is not a denial of justice but an act of spiritual obedience, one that reflects God's character and allows His love to work through us. Jesus reminds us to forgive not just once but "seventy times seven." This commitment to forgiveness invites us to actively pursue reconciliation, trusting God to rebuild what bitterness has destroyed. Each act of grace—no matter how small—creates ripples of healing and hope, inviting God's presence into our communities and institutions.

RIVERS OF LIVING WATER

Jesus' prayer from the cross, Father, forgive them, for they know not what they do, stands as the ultimate example of forgiveness in the face of pain and injustice. His words resonate with divine love, showing us that forgiveness is not dependent on the offender's actions but on God's grace working within us. Forgiveness breaks the chains of resentment and builds bridges of unity, paving the way for communities and institutions to reflect God's love. When we forgive, we step into the work of Christ, healing fractures and inspiring trust within our state.

The Holy Spirit enables us to forgive even when the hurt feels insurmountable. He softens our hardened hearts, replacing anger with compassion and reminding us of the boundless grace we have received. Forgiveness, empowered by the Spirit, is not passive; it's an active choice to reflect God's love. Whether it's reconciling with a neighbor or advocating for systemic changes that promote justice, forgiveness becomes a powerful channel for God's work. Isaiah 1:18 reminds us, "though your sins are like scarlet, they shall be as white as snow." Through the Spirit, forgiveness transforms our hearts and the communities we touch.

Forgiveness begins with prayer and leads to action. Ask God for the courage to release anger and offer grace. Pray for those who have wronged you, but also take tangible steps to mend broken relationships or support reconciliation efforts. Advocate for policies in your state that prioritize restorative justice over punishment, trusting that God can use your obedience to inspire healing. Forgiveness is like a stone dropped into a still pond—each act of grace sends ripples outward, impacting hearts, relationships, and institutions with God's transformative power.

DEEP CALLS TO DEEP

Who in your life mirrors the fractured bonds we see in our state's communities? Forgiveness is not just for the offender; it's a balm for your soul. By taking the first step—whether through prayer or a courageous conversation—you invite God's grace to bridge even the deepest divides. Picture bitterness as a chain: every act of forgiveness is a link broken, setting both parties free to embrace His healing love.

Heart Prayer

Dear Heavenly Father,

May Your peace and grace flow freely through our state, replacing resentment with understanding and love. Heal the divisions that fracture relationships and communities. May Your Spirit guide us to extend forgiveness without hesitation, creating an environment where trust and unity can thrive. Fill our hearts with Your love and make them instruments of Your grace. Amen.

Soul Prayer

Lord Jesus,

Teach us to follow Your example of forgiveness, even when it feels difficult. Help us release grudges and embrace grace, shaping our communities into reflections of Your kingdom. Transform our souls with compassion, inspiring us to seek unity over division. May our actions mirror Your love and bring healing to every corner of our state. Amen.

Mind Prayer

Holy Spirit,

Grant us the wisdom to approach conflicts with both clarity and compassion. Help us respond in ways that embody Your peace and foster reconciliation among those around us. Equip us to serve as instruments of unity, bringing harmony to a world often torn by division.

Strength Prayer

God Three-in-One,

Empower us to forgive when the pain feels overwhelming. Give us the strength to extend grace where it is most needed, rebuilding trust and restoring unity. Use our lives as vessels of Your forgiveness, creating communities where Your love reigns. May our actions glorify You as we live out the call to reconciliation.

For Thine is the kingdom, Lord Jesus
Thine is the power, Holy Spirit
And Thine is the glory, Heavenly Father,
forever. Amen.

~

God's presence fills the spaces where we invite Him to dwell, bringing peace and healing. Each act of love— whether through forgiveness, generosity, or kindness— becomes a testimony to His grace. Today, ask Him to guide you in creating meaningful connections with those around you. Trust that your faithfulness will reflect His light and inspire hope in unexpected ways.

NOTES:

DAY 23

Restoring Relationships in Our Nation

*And forgive us our debts, as we also
have forgiven our debtors.*
(Matthew 6:12, HCSB)

The expanse of our nation's mountains, rivers, and plains mirrors the diversity of its people and the challenges that arise when differing perspectives collide. Forgiveness, though often viewed as weakness, is a courageous act of strength that mends wounds, rebuilds trust, and invites God's grace to restore fractured relationships. Forgiveness may feel like surrendering justice, but it creates a justice rooted in grace and healing. Like soft rain on parched earth, it refreshes and renews, making space for unity to flourish.

BESIDE QUIET WATERS

Picture a nation where forgiveness transcends being an ideal and becomes a living reality. Its citizens intentionally choose unity over division, joining hands to heal even the deepest wounds. This powerful vision begins with each individual responding to God's call to forgive, embodying His grace in every interaction and relationship.

God invites us to build our relationships on the solid foundation of forgiveness. By choosing to forgive, we mirror His love and release the burdens of bitterness that weigh us down. This transformative act not only heals relationships but also draws us closer to the heart of God, deepening our connection with Him and others.

The world often demands retribution and holds tight to grudges, but God's way invites us to a higher path. Forgiveness does not negate accountability; rather, it provides an avenue for grace to coexist with justice. Jesus' teaching to forgive "seventy times seven" reminds us that forgiveness is a lifestyle, not a single act. Let each step toward grace—whether in personal relationships or national systems—send ripples of hope, healing what bitterness has broken and inspiring others to choose love over division.

RIVERS OF LIVING WATER

Jesus demonstrated forgiveness in its purest form as He endured the cross. His prayer, "Father, forgive them, for they know not what they do" [Luke 23:34], reflects divine love that reaches beyond betrayal and pain. Forgiveness was not a sign of weakness; it was a powerful declaration of God's grace. Imagine the transformation if this same forgiveness flowed through our nation, healing brokenness and uniting communities. Each act of grace becomes a bridge, leading hearts to reconciliation and hope.

The Holy Spirit equips us to forgive when we feel incapable. He softens our hardened hearts, replacing anger with compassion, and reminds us of the immeasurable grace we've received. Through His power, forgiveness moves from obligation to opportunity, becoming a reflection of God's heart. Romans 5:8 reminds us, "While we were still sinners, Christ died for us." Just as God initiated forgiveness toward us, we are called to extend it toward others. Forgiveness, though difficult, opens doors for God's healing work in our lives and our nation.

Forgiveness requires both prayer and intentional action. Begin by asking God to help you release resentment and seek reconciliation. Consider writing a letter of forgiveness to someone who has wronged you, even if it's never sent. Support organizations in your nation that promote reconciliation and address systemic injustices. Through these steps, you reflect God's love and inspire others to do the same. Forgiveness, like a planted seed, bears fruit that nourishes future generations, transforming relationships and systems alike.

DEEP CALLS TO DEEP

Forgiveness is the foundation upon which reconciliation is built. As you enter prayer, reflect on how the words, "And forgive us our debts, as we also have forgiven our debtors," resonate in your life and your nation. Are there relationships, communities, or institutions in need of healing? Trust that God's grace is sufficient to transform even the deepest wounds, using your prayers and actions to inspire reconciliation and renewal.

Heart Prayer

Dear Heavenly Father,

May Your peace saturate our nation. Replace resentment with understanding and division with unity. Heal the wounds of past injustices and inspire forgiveness in every heart. May our nation reflect Your grace as we extend forgiveness to others. Teach us to forgive as You have forgiven us, allowing Your love to transform every broken place. Amen.

Soul Prayer

Lord Jesus,

Teach us to follow Your example of boundless forgiveness. Transform our hearts with compassion, enabling us to release anger and extend grace. Let our nation reflect Your kingdom as we pursue unity and reconciliation. Guide us to be ambassadors of Your peace, bringing healing wherever we go. Amen.

Mind Prayer

Holy Spirit,

Grant us wisdom to navigate conflicts with clarity and humility. Help us to see others through Your eyes, offering forgiveness and understanding. Fill our minds with Your Word, shaping our decisions and interactions to reflect Your truth. May Your guidance lead our nation toward unity and peace. Amen.

Strength Prayer

God Three-in-One,

Empower us to forgive with courage and humility. Strengthen us to rebuild trust and extend grace, even when it feels impossible. Use our lives as vessels of Your forgiveness, creating communities where Your love reigns. May our actions inspire healing and glorify You in all we do.

For Thine is the kingdom, Lord Jesus Thine is the power, Holy Spirit And Thine is the glory, Heavenly Father, forever. Amen.

~

God's peace flows into our lives when we make room for His presence, allowing Him to shape our thoughts, words, and actions. Each time you trust Him with your burdens or choose to show kindness, you reflect His grace to those around you. Today, pause and consider how your life can become a channel for His healing power—whether by offering a listening ear, praying for someone in need, or bringing comfort to a weary heart. These simple acts of love carry His peace into places longing for renewal. Trust that as you surrender to Him, He will use you to bring restoration and hope, one step of faith at a time.

DAY 24

Restoring Relationships in Our World

*And forgive us our debts, as we also
have forgiven our debtors.
(Matthew 6:12, NASB)*

The intricate mosaic of creation reveals the unmistakable handiwork of the Creator. Each unique and purposeful thread is woven together to form a magnificent masterpiece that reflects His divine design. By recognizing God's artistry, we are inspired to embrace our unique roles, contributing to His masterpiece with faith and gratitude.

BESIDE QUIET WATERS

Imagine forgiveness flowing like a mighty river, cutting paths of healing through deserts of hatred and fields of injustice. In the aftermath of a civil war, two nations established a Truth and Reconciliation Commission. Victims and offenders shared their stories with raw honesty, and voices that had once been silenced rose together in forgiveness. This courageous act became a foundation for trust, cooperation, and lasting peace. Forgiveness is not a single act but a mighty current that carves new landscapes of hope.

God's desire for our world is to see forgiveness transcend borders, healing wounds and uniting people. The Shema reminds us to love God with all our heart, soul, mind, and strength. This love finds its expression in grace extended to others, in forgiveness that mirrors Christ's gift to us. Imagine a world where nations seek reconciliation rather than retaliation, where leaders embrace mercy over vengeance, and where every act of grace ripples outward, shaping a more compassionate global community.

The world glorifies vengeance, yet God calls us to choose forgiveness. Forgiveness is not about denying justice; it is about allowing God's grace to triumph. Each act of forgiveness becomes a bridge between pain and peace. Jesus' command to forgive seventy times seven invites us into a rhythm of reconciliation that transforms relationships, systems, and hearts.

RIVERS OF LIVING WATER

Jesus crossed boundaries of culture and status to extend forgiveness and healing. His prayer on the cross, "Father, forgive them, for they know not what they do" (Luke 23:34), exemplifies the ultimate act of love and grace. Forgiveness is not the absence of accountability; it is the presence of God's redemptive love. Imagine nations embracing this spirit of forgiveness, allowing peace to flow into every corner of the earth.

The Holy Spirit equips us to forgive when it feels beyond our capacity. He reshapes anger into compassion, empowering us to see others through the lens of God's grace. Romans 12:18 reminds us, "If possible, so far as it depends on you, be at peace with all men." The Spirit helps us move beyond grievances to pursue reconciliation. Whether addressing personal wounds or historical injustices, forgiveness becomes an instrument of God's transformative power.

Forgiveness calls for prayer and action. Begin with prayer, asking God to reveal areas where forgiveness is needed in your life or community. Consider writing a letter of forgiveness to someone who has hurt you, even if you never send it. Support global organizations working to heal cultural and political divides. As Isaiah 58:12 declares, "You will be called Repairer of Broken Walls, Restorer of Streets with Dwellings." Each step taken in forgiveness reflects God's redemptive love and lays a foundation for peace.

DEEP CALLS TO DEEP

Forgiveness is the bridge between brokenness and healing. As you pray, reflect on the words, "And forgive us our debts, as we also have forgiven our debtors." Ask God to reveal areas where forgiveness can bring renewal and unity in your world. Trust that His grace is sufficient to transform even the deepest divides.

Heart Prayer

> *Dear Heavenly Father,*
>
> *Fill our world with Your peace. Replace bitterness with understanding and*

division with reconciliation. Heal the wounds of the past and restore trust among nations and communities. Teach us to forgive as You have forgiven us, allowing Your love to bring hope and unity. Amen.

Soul Prayer

Lord Jesus,

Help us follow Your example of forgiveness. Inspire leaders to seek reconciliation and guide us to reflect Your grace in every interaction. Transform our hearts to release anger and embrace compassion. May our world become a reflection of Your kingdom, united by Your love. Amen.

Mind Prayer

Holy Spirit,

Grant us wisdom to approach conflict with humility and understanding. Help us see others through Your eyes and respond with grace. May Your Word shape our thoughts and guide our actions toward peace and reconciliation. Open our minds to solutions that bring healing across cultures and nations. Amen.

Strength Prayer

God Three-in-One,

Strengthen us to forgive boldly and consistently. Empower us to release resentment and work for restoration. Use us as instruments of Your love to mend broken relationships and inspire unity. Let our lives reflect Your forgiveness and glorify Your name.

For Thine is the kingdom, Lord Jesus
Thine is the power, Holy Spirit
And Thine is the glory, Heavenly Father,
forever. Amen.

~

God's character is reflected in how we live, serve, and love others, shaping the world around us with His truth. Every decision to extend grace or act in faith creates opportunities for His glory to shine. Today, take a moment to invite Him into the choices you face, allowing His wisdom to guide you toward love and unity. Through the smallest gestures—a word of encouragement, a prayer for a friend, or an act of service—you reveal His heart to a watching world. Trust that as you remain faithful, God will use your obedience to inspire transformation in ways you cannot yet imagine. Let His presence in your life bring His hope to others today.

NOTES:

DAY 25

God's Protection in Our Home

And lead us not into temptation,
but deliver us from evil.
(Matthew 6:13, KJV)

Our homes are havens where we seek refuge from the world's pressures, yet they are also battlegrounds for spiritual challenges. Jesus' words, "And lead us not into temptation, but deliver us from evil," speak directly to our need for God's protection in these intimate spaces. Temptation is a thread woven into humanity's story, but God offers His strength to overcome it. His protection surrounds us like the walls of an ancient fortress, steadfast and secure against the schemes of the enemy.

BESIDE QUIET WATERS

Picture a family facing a storm of anxiety—perhaps financial strain or relational tension. As fears threaten to consume them, they gather in their living room to pray. The soft murmur of their voices rises with words of trust and surrender, and the atmosphere shifts. Peace replaces fear as they cling to God's promises. Challenges remain, but the family's faith becomes a shield, reminding them of God's unfailing presence and power.

God desires our homes to be fortresses of faith, places where His truth reigns and His peace guards every corner. Just as the Shema calls us to love God with all our heart, soul, mind, and strength, this love takes shape in homes anchored by prayer, Scripture, and trust in His protection. These spiritual disciplines create a rhythm of faithfulness, shielding our homes from the temptations that threaten to destabilize them.

The world entices us to pursue self-sufficiency and fleeting pleasures, but God calls us to a higher standard. Temptation does not vanish, but He equips us to resist. Clothed in the armor of God, we stand united as families, hallowing His name through our reliance on Him. Each prayer, each act of obedience, becomes a testimony to His protection and a shining light of His presence in our homes.

RIVERS OF LIVING WATER

Jesus' victory over temptation in the wilderness offers a powerful example of relying on God's Word in the face of trials. Prayer anchored His heart, and Scripture fortified His mind, enabling Him to stand against the enemy. This same power is available to us. Prayer becomes our anchor, steadying us in the storms of temptation, while God's Word is the sword that equips us to stand firm.

The Holy Spirit empowers us to resist temptation, guiding us toward truth and righteousness. He convicts us of sin, illuminates the path of obedience, and transforms our hearts with God's promises. His presence reminds us that we are never alone in our struggles. As 1 Corinthians 10:13 declares, "God is faithful; He will not let you be tempted beyond what you can bear. But when you are tempted, He will also provide a way out so that you can endure it." The Spirit's strength enables us to walk in victory, even when the challenges feel overwhelming.

Building a steady rhythm of spiritual disciplines establishes a firm foundation for a life anchored in God's peace. Through consistent practices like prayer, Scripture study, and mindful reflection, our hearts become attuned to His divine purposes. This alignment with God's will empowers us to navigate uncertainties with wisdom, grace, and enduring faith.

DEEP CALLS TO DEEP

Prayer is the doorway to God's protection. Reflect on the words, "And lead us not into temptation, but deliver us from evil." Where does your home need His presence most? Invite Him into every vulnerable place, trusting His strength to guide, protect, and restore.

Heart Prayer

Dear Heavenly Father,

Fill our home with Your peace and shield us from the schemes of the enemy. Guard our hearts against fear and temptation, anchoring us in Your truth. May our home be a haven where Your presence is felt, and Your love flows freely. Teach us to trust

You fully, knowing that You are our refuge and strength. Amen.

Soul Prayer

Lord Jesus,

Help us depend on You for protection and guidance. Strengthen our relationships with Your love, teaching us to support one another through prayer and encouragement. Transform our hearts to resist temptation and to walk in obedience to Your Word. May our family honor You in every thought, word, and action. Amen.

Mind Prayer

Holy Spirit,

Grant us wisdom to recognize and resist the enemy's schemes. Guard our thoughts with Your truth and fill our minds with Your Word. Help us discern what honors You and choose paths that reflect Your righteousness. May our home be a place where Your wisdom reigns and Your guidance is sought daily. Amen.

Strength Prayer

God Three-in-One,

*Empower us to stand strong against
temptation and to overcome adversity
with faith. Fill us with courage to trust
You in every challenge, knowing that Your
power sustains us. May our home be a
testimony to Your strength and grace,
inspiring others to seek refuge in You.*

*For Thine is the kingdom, Lord Jesus
Thine is the power, Holy Spirit
And Thine is the glory, Heavenly Father,
forever. Amen.*

~

Peace unfolds when we surrender our fears and trust in God's steady hand. Each act of faith—whether offering comfort to a friend, choosing patience over frustration, or sharing an encouraging word—becomes a reflection of His love. Look for ways today to carry His peace into the spaces you inhabit, letting His presence guide your responses and renew your heart. As you align your steps with His promises, believe that even the smallest gestures can bring healing and hope to others. Trust that God is at work, using your faithfulness to bring restoration to lives in need of His grace.

DAY 26

God's Protection in Our Neighborhood

And lead us not into temptation,
but deliver us from the evil one.
(Matthew 6:13, NIV)

Neighborhoods are vibrant tapestries woven with moments of connection, challenge, and grace. In these shared spaces, the words of the Lord's Prayer, And lead us not into temptation, but deliver us from the evil one, resonate deeply. This plea reminds us of our need for God's protection, urging us to trust Him as our ever-watchful Shepherd, guiding and shielding us from harm. God's presence transforms our neighborhoods into sanctuaries of safety, where His peace guards our hearts and minds.

BESIDE QUIET WATERS

Picture a neighborhood facing unrest—a season of rising tensions, crime, and fear. In response, a group of neighbors gathers weekly to pray for God's protection and renewal.

Through their united faith, new initiatives emerge: a neighborhood watch program, meal trains for families in need, and a deep commitment to care for one another. One night, as a young woman walks home alone, she faces a moment of terror when strangers surround her. Just then, a porch light blazes, and a neighbor calls out, scattering her would-be attackers. The light becomes more than a physical rescue—it is a reminder of God's providence and His power to deliver.

God desires neighborhoods to reflect His kingdom, where peace triumphs over fear and love replaces indifference. The Shema's call to love Him with all our heart, soul, mind, and strength extends to how we engage with others, transforming our streets into places of shared safety and hope. In these small, faithful acts of love and protection, His light shines, revealing that no darkness can extinguish His truth.

The world often whispers that self-reliance and isolation are the safest paths. God calls us instead to step into faith, building bridges of connection and living boldly as His ambassadors. Through His strength, our neighborhoods become places where trust grows, compassion multiplies, and His protection is powerfully felt.

RIVERS OF LIVING WATER

Jesus sought out the vulnerable and the overlooked, offering compassion and restoration to those others avoided. His ministry reminds us that God's love knows no bounds, and His protection is available to all. Just as Jesus walked among those in need, offering healing and hope, we are called to engage our neighbors with that same intentional care, showing the transformative power of His love.

Imagine a neighborhood where people truly see one another—where kindness replaces suspicion and generosity bridges gaps. The Holy Spirit empowers us to break down barriers of fear and prejudice, filling our hearts with a compassion that reflects God's image in every person we meet. This Spirit-led love moves us to pray for our neighbors, discern their needs, and act with grace to bring His peace into their lives.

Through prayer and action, God calls us to engage fully with heart, soul, mind, and strength. Begin by creating a rhythm of intercession for your community, lifting up those who are burdened and seeking ways to serve the marginalized. Offer hospitality to the lonely, forgiveness to the estranged, and encouragement to the weary. Let your presence in your neighborhood become a testimony of God's unchanging love and unshakable protection.

DEEP CALLS TO DEEP

When we pray, "And lead us not into temptation, but deliver us from the evil one," we acknowledge the reality of spiritual battles in our neighborhoods. Are there areas in your community where fear has taken root? Are there families in need of God's protection or individuals who feel trapped by temptation? These are invitations to call upon the Lord, who is our refuge and strength. He longs to bring peace where there is conflict and light where shadows loom.

Heart Prayer

Dear Heavenly Father,

Bring peace to our neighborhoods and replace fear with Your confidence. Protect us from temptation and shield us from the enemy's schemes. May Your presence shine brightly in every corner, filling our streets with hope and safety. Amen.

Soul Prayer

Lord Jesus,

Open our neighbors' hearts to recognize their need for You. Strengthen our resolve to resist temptation and guide us to live in obedience to Your Word. Align our lives with Your will, that we may honor You through love and service. Amen.

Mind Prayer

Holy Spirit,

Grant us wisdom to discern the enemy's strategies and courage to act on Your truth. Guard our thoughts against harmful influences and fill our minds with the richness of Your Word. May Your truth reign in our neighborhoods, bringing renewal and joy. Amen.

Strength Prayer

God Three-in-One,

Empower us to resist temptation with boldness and grace. Strengthen us to reflect Your power in every action and fill our neighborhoods with Your protective presence. May our lives bear witness to Your unshakable strength.

For Thine is the kingdom, Lord Jesus
Thine is the power, Holy Spirit
And Thine is the glory, Heavenly Father,
forever. Amen.

~

In every moment, God offers us the chance to reflect His grace and love to the world around us. Whether through a heartfelt prayer, an encouraging word, or a quiet act of service, your actions carry His presence into the lives of others. Today, consider how you can live in a way that points to His faithfulness—be it through mending a strained relationship, meeting a need, or simply showing kindness. Each step of obedience opens the door for His light to shine brighter. Trust that as you act in faith, God will use your efforts to bring healing and hope far beyond what you can see.

NOTES:

DAY 27

God's Protection in Our Community

Keep us from being tempted and protect us from evil. (Matthew 6:13, CEV)

Communities, like living ecosystems, are woven with moments of connection, challenge, and renewal. The Lord's Prayer anchors us with the words, "Keep us from being tempted and protect us from evil." This plea is both a confession of our vulnerability and a declaration of trust in God's power to shield us. His protection is our harbor in life's storms, guarding us against the currents of fear and temptation.

BESIDE QUIET WATERS

In a small town once divided by economic struggles, misunderstandings multiplied, and trust eroded. A coalition of churches took bold action, uniting to create mentoring programs and community gardens. Prayer walks became a weekly rhythm, and neighbors began to share meals and stories. Over time, the barriers of fear and mistrust crumbled. One young boy, mentored through this initiative, said, "This place feels safe now, like God is here." His words reflect the transformation that happens when God's protection is welcomed into the heart of a community.

God envisions our communities as reflections of His kingdom, where love triumphs over fear and unity overcomes division. The Shema commands us to love God with all our heart, soul, mind, and strength—a love that compels us to act with compassion and integrity. By standing together in His strength, we create havens of safety and belonging where His light shines brightly.

The world whispers that isolation and self-reliance are the best defenses, yet God offers a better way. When we hallow His name in our communities, we step into a partnership with His protection. By choosing faith over fear, we embody His love in ways that transform lives and neighborhoods.

RIVERS OF LIVING WATER

Jesus showed us the power of compassionate action through His ministry. He sought out those marginalized by society, restoring their dignity and inviting them into the embrace of God's love. His life teaches us that God's protection is not only a shield but also an invitation to reflect His care to others.

The Holy Spirit empowers us to respond to life's challenges with wisdom and compassion, embodying the heart of Christ. By guiding our decisions and fortifying our resolve, He ensures that our actions align with God's will. Through

His presence, we are equipped to reflect Christ's love and grace in every circumstance.

Engaging our whole selves—heart, soul, mind, and strength—invites God's transformative power into our communities. By lifting up neighbors in prayer, creating safe spaces for connection, and extending kindness to the vulnerable, we reflect His light and protection in ways that draw others closer to Him.

DEEP CALLS TO DEEP

The words, "Keep us from being tempted and protect us from evil," remind us that God's protection is a promise for every aspect of life. Reflect on the areas of your community that most need His intervention. Are there tensions, fears, or struggles that feel insurmountable? Trust that He is our refuge and strength, present and powerful in every need.

Heart Prayer

> *Dear Heavenly Father,*
>
> *Bring Your peace into every corner of our communities. May Your love transform fear into trust and replace isolation with connection. Protect us from the temptations that divide and from the evils that threaten unity. May Your presence draw us into deeper reliance on You and may Your light shine through every act of kindness. Amen.*

Soul Prayer

Lord Jesus,

Open our neighbors' hearts to Your grace. May we live in ways that reflect Your love and inspire others to seek You. May our lives testify to Your protection, creating a ripple of hope and renewal across our community. Amen.

Mind Prayer

Holy Spirit,

Grant us discernment to navigate the challenges that arise. May Your truth guide our decisions, and Your grace shape our words. Teach us to protect what is good and just, reflecting Your wisdom in our communities. Amen.

Strength Prayer

God Three-in-One,

Equip us to stand firm in the face of adversity, resisting temptation and walking boldly in faith. Strengthen us to be protectors of the vulnerable and advocates for peace. May our lives reflect Your love and power, bringing safety and unity to our neighborhoods.

For Thine is the kingdom, Lord Jesus
Thine is the power, Holy Spirit
And Thine is the glory, Heavenly Father,
forever. Amen.

~

Surrendering fully to God unlocks His power to restore and renew. With every step of faith, whether small or bold, His Spirit brings light into the hidden corners of our world. Reflect on how you can serve today, offering kindness or a word of hope where it is needed most. Trust that even your simplest actions can be used by Him to heal brokenness and inspire change. As you follow His lead, you'll see His love working through you in ways far beyond what you can envision. Let each moment be a testimony to His presence and a catalyst for His kingdom's growth.

NOTES:

DAY 28

God's Protection in Our State

And lead us not into temptation
but deliver us from evil.
(Matthew 6:13, KJV)

From its vibrant cities to its rolling farmlands, every corner of our state carries its own challenges and beauty. The Lord's Prayer anchors us in the words, And lead us not into temptation, but deliver us from evil, reminding us to seek God's protection for all aspects of life. His presence shields us from harm and fortifies us to resist temptation, empowering us to live as agents of His truth and love.

BESIDE QUIET WATERS

In a state plagued by corruption, faithful believers united in prayer, calling on God to intervene. They asked Him to raise up leaders of integrity who would honor justice. Their prayers became the seeds of change. Stories emerged of courageous legislators enacting reforms that prioritized ethics over ambition. Citizens were inspired to demand transparency, and communities joined together to uphold truth. This movement, like rivers of hope flowing through valleys of despair, testified to the transformative power of prayer and God's faithfulness to protect and guide.

God's vision for states reflects His kingdom values—justice, compassion, and integrity. The Shema reminds us to love God with all our heart, soul, mind, and strength, extending this love into every policy and relationship. Imagine a state where leaders govern with humility and communities thrive in unity. Such a place reflects His righteousness and invites His protection over its people.

The world often glorifies self-interest and compromise, tempting us to abandon truth for convenience. God calls us higher, urging us to hallow His name through integrity and faith. By standing firm in His power, we become vessels of His peace, illuminating every corner of our state with His light and love.

RIVERS OF LIVING WATER

Jesus demonstrated unwavering trust in God's plan, even in the face of profound suffering. His complete surrender to the Father's will paved the way for salvation to reach all of humanity. His example inspires us to embrace courage, trusting in God's purposes even when they surpass our understanding.

The Holy Spirit equips us to discern areas in our state that need healing and transformation. He stirs us to act with wisdom and courage, addressing the root causes of poverty, injustice, and division. In one struggling town, a group of mothers started meeting weekly for prayer. Their prayers led to community mentoring programs, safety initiatives, and advocacy for policies that protected vulnerable families. These Spirit-led actions became shining lights of God's protection, illuminating paths of restoration and renewal.

Engaging our whole selves—heart, soul, mind, and strength—in prayer and action invites God's presence into every facet of our state. Begin by praying for leaders to govern with wisdom and integrity. Seek opportunities to serve through advocacy or volunteer work that reflects His justice. Each act, no matter how small, becomes a tangible expression of His love, creating ripples that bring His protection and peace to the broken places around us.

DEEP CALLS TO DEEP

The words, "And lead us not into temptation, but deliver us from evil," remind us to intercede fervently for God's protection over our state. Reflect on the leaders, systems, and families that need His guidance. Trust that as we pray and act in faith, He will bring healing, justice, and peace to every area of need.

Heart Prayer

Dear Heavenly Father,

Fill our state with Your peace and protect us from the enemy's schemes. Guard the hearts of leaders and citizens against the temptations of greed and division. Unite us in Your truth and guide us to reflect Your love in every action. May Your presence transform our state into a sanctuary of justice and hope. Amen.

Soul Prayer

Lord Jesus,

Open the hearts of leaders and citizens to Your truth. Help us walk in obedience to Your Word and inspire us to be bold witnesses of Your love. Transform our communities into places where compassion and unity flourish, reflecting Your kingdom on earth. Amen.

Mind Prayer

Holy Spirit,

Grant wisdom to our leaders to make decisions that align with Your truth. Help us discern the enemy's lies and replace them with Your Word. Let our thoughts and actions reflect Your justice and mercy, bringing renewal to every corner of our state. Amen.

Strength Prayer

God Three-in-One,

Strengthen us to stand firm in faith and persevere in prayer and action. Empower us to confront injustice with boldness and grace. Let our state thrive under Your care, reflecting Your glory and bringing hope to generations.

For Thine is the kingdom, Lord Jesus
Thine is the power, Holy Spirit
And Thine is the glory, Heavenly Father,
forever. Amen.

~

Transformation begins when we invite God into the ordinary moments of our lives. Each choice to forgive, serve, or encourage becomes an act of worship, revealing His grace to those around us. Today, think about how your actions can reflect His love—whether it's reaching out to someone in need, offering a prayer for guidance, or extending compassion where it's least expected. Through these steps of faith, His peace flows into your life and touches others. Trust that God is working through you, creating opportunities for His presence to bring healing and hope in ways you may not yet see.

NOTES:

DAY 29

God's Protection in Our Nation

And lead us not into temptation
but deliver us from the evil one.
(Matthew 6:13, NIV)

The spiritual and moral challenges within our nation call believers to fervent prayer. Jesus' words, "And lead us not into temptation, but deliver us from the evil one," emphasize the power of seeking God's protection. This prayer serves as both a shield against darkness and a declaration of faith in God's ability to lead us through trials. Prayers offered on behalf of a nation invite God's light to guide and transform every corner of society.

BESIDE QUIET WATERS

During a national crisis, a dedicated group of intercessors responded with fervent prayer and fasting. Their unwavering devotion not only sparked transformative change but also stood as a powerful testimony to the strength of faith. Through their steadfast commitment, they illuminated the boundless possibilities of lives fully surrendered to God's purpose and power.

God envisions a nation aligned with His kingdom values— justice for all, love for neighbors, and truth in every sphere. The Shema instructs believers to love God fully, reflecting this love in every aspect of life. A nation rooted in such devotion honors Him through integrity, humility, and faith. By seeking His protection and acting with courage, believers can illuminate pathways of renewal and hope.

The world often promotes power and self-interest as solutions to its deepest problems. God calls His people to a better way, one defined by humility and prayer. Through obedience and faith, believers can reflect His character and invite His presence to dwell in their nation.

RIVERS OF LIVING WATER

The ministry of Jesus unveiled the transformative power of God's boundless love and grace. He reached out to heal the broken, restore the lost, and embrace the marginalized. In every encounter, He revealed that every individual is of infinite worth to God, reflecting the depth of His compassion and care.

The Holy Spirit empowers believers with the wisdom to discern God's will and the strength to follow it faithfully. He equips us to face challenges with courage and to proclaim the Gospel boldly and clearly. This divine power transforms everyday lives into extraordinary vessels of purpose, bringing glory to God through faithful obedience.

Prayers joined with action bring tangible expressions of God's love into the world. Advocating for justice, standing with the marginalized, and encouraging leaders who uphold truth are ways to participate in God's redemptive work. Faithful believers, acting with heart, soul, mind, and strength, reflect His light in every aspect of national life.

DEEP CALLS TO DEEP

The prayer, "And lead us not into temptation, but deliver us from the evil one," is a call to seek God's guidance and protection for our nation. Reflect on the specific areas where His light is needed most. Interceding for leaders, systems, and communities brings hope and renewal as we trust in His power to act.

Heart Prayer

Dear Heavenly Father,

Protect our nation and fill it with Your peace. Guard the hearts of leaders against pride and selfishness and guide their decisions toward righteousness. May Your love unite us, and may Your presence transform every corner of our nation into a sanctuary of hope and justice. Amen.

Soul Prayer

Lord Jesus,

Awaken the hearts of our nation's people to their need for You. Strengthen our resolve to walk in obedience to Your Word and reflect Your love in every interaction. Let our lives serve as testimonies of Your grace

and truth, inspiring others to seek You.
Amen.

Mind Prayer

Holy Spirit,

Grant wisdom to our leaders and clarity to those navigating difficult decisions. Help us discern truth and act with courage, inspired by Your Word. May Your guidance shape policies and actions, creating a nation rooted in justice and mercy. Amen.

Strength Prayer

God Three-in-One,

Empower us to resist the pull of apathy and to stand boldly for righteousness. Strengthen us to serve others with humility and courage. May Your power sustain us in every endeavor as we seek to glorify Your name through our prayers and actions.

For Thine is the kingdom, Lord Jesus
Thine is the power, Holy Spirit
And Thine is the glory, Heavenly Father,
forever. Amen.

~

Every act of trust in God allows His truth to shine through your life. When you choose to love generously, speak with kindness, or extend forgiveness, you create space for His peace to transform hearts. Reflect today on how you can align your thoughts and actions with His will, stepping out in faith even in the smallest of ways. These moments, shaped by obedience, can ripple outward to inspire healing and restoration. Believe that God's presence will use your faithfulness to touch lives, spreading His hope and grace wherever He leads you.

NOTES:

DAY 30

God's Protection in Our World

Keep us from being tempted and
protect us from evil.
(Matthew 6:13, CEV)

The world carries breathtaking beauty alongside deep brokenness. Jesus' words, "And do not lead us into temptation, but deliver us from evil," serve as a steadfast anchor for the challenges humanity faces. This prayer acknowledges our daily battles and our dependence on God's sovereign power to guard and restore. His protection extends beyond physical safety to spiritual renewal, shielding hearts and minds from the schemes of the enemy. As we intercede for the world, we declare trust in His transformative love to bring peace where there is chaos and light where shadows linger.

BESIDE QUIET WATERS

A powerful story emerged from a war-torn region where fear gripped communities, and hope seemed far away. A small group of believers began gathering each week to pray for God's protection and intervention. Their intercession, like threads of heaven stitching hope into a weary world, became the foundation for change. Miracles followed: ceasefires brought reprieve, humanitarian aid arrived, and displaced families found safety. Beyond the physical restoration, spiritual awakening swept through the land. People turned to Christ, finding refuge and peace amid the uncertainty. This testimony of prayer's power challenges us to lift our world to God, trusting Him to intervene in ways beyond human understanding.

God's ultimate act of deliverance came through Jesus, who conquered evil and made eternal life possible. He longs for the nations to thrive under His protection—not just from harm, but from spiritual decay. The Shema calls us to love God with all our heart, soul, mind, and strength. This love compels us to pray for nations, advocate for the persecuted, and reflect His justice and mercy in our own communities. Imagine a world where leaders seek God's wisdom, nations embody His peace, and His presence brings healing to the most broken places. This vision can become reality as we partner with Him through prayer and faithful action.

The world offers solutions rooted in power, wealth, and human strength, but God calls us to a better way. Through prayer and acts of compassion, we amplify His light in the darkest places. Supporting justice advocates, engaging in relief efforts, and modeling His love bring His presence into the world's deepest needs. Each prayer and action become part of His redemptive story, revealing His protection and provision for a world desperate for hope.

RIVERS OF LIVING WATER

The ministry of Jesus unveiled the infinite power and unmatched compassion of God. He reached out to the sick, offering healing; He comforted those burdened by grief, and brought hope to the brokenhearted. In every act, He revealed that no one stands outside the encompassing reach of God's love, reaffirming His desire to restore and redeem all who come to Him.

The Holy Spirit empowers believers to pray with boldness, transforming fear into faith. He grants discernment to see the needs of the world and guides prayers that align with God's will. Each answered prayer becomes a bridge of hope, testifying to His faithfulness and reinforcing trust in His protection. One example of this was seen in a small prayer group interceding for a neighboring country during a humanitarian crisis. Their prayers inspired donations, relief efforts, and advocacy that led to tangible change for those in need. These moments of Spirit-led action magnify God's power, proving that prayer moves hearts and history.

Engaging fully in global prayer and service calls for heart, soul, mind, and strength. Pray for nations in conflict, the persecuted Church, and leaders to act with integrity and compassion. Support missionaries, advocate for justice, and contribute to humanitarian aid. Through faith in action, we become living testimonies of God's love and protection. Every step taken in obedience reflects His light in a hurting world, reminding us that He remains our refuge and strength.

DEEP CALLS TO DEEP

The prayer, "Deliver us from evil," reminds us of the urgent need for God's protection across the world. Intercession brings His power into situations beyond our reach, aligning our hearts with His will. Reflect on the areas where the world most needs His intervention and trust Him to work through your prayers.

Heart Prayer

> *Dear Heavenly Father,*
>
> *We lift the world to You. Protect the vulnerable, bring comfort to the grieving, and heal communities torn by conflict. Guard leaders against the temptation of pride and greed and guide them toward justice and humility. Transform hearts to seek Your peace, and let Your love be known in every nation. Amen.*

Soul Prayer

> *Lord Jesus,*
>
> *Open hearts to Your guidance and truth. Strengthen us to resist temptation and empower us to walk faithfully in obedience to Your Word. May Your mercy flow through us, inspiring others to turn to You. May Your Spirit renew the world, creating*

unity and hope in places of division.
Amen.

Mind Prayer

Holy Spirit,

Illuminate our minds with wisdom as we
pray for the world. Show us where to focus
our prayers and guide our thoughts to
align with Your truth. Help us discern the
schemes of the enemy and speak boldly
against injustice. Fill us with faith in Your
promises and courage to advocate for the
oppressed. Amen.

Strength Prayer

God Three-in-One,

Grant us courage to face global challenges
with boldness and grace. Strengthen us to
act in love, bringing hope to those in
despair. Equip us to persevere in prayer
and service, trusting in Your power to do
exceedingly more than we can imagine.
May Your protection and provision shine
through our efforts, revealing Your glory
to the nations.

For Thine is the kingdom, Lord Jesus
Thine is the power, Holy Spirit

And Thine is the glory, Heavenly Father,
forever. Amen.

~

Living a life shaped by God's love transforms both your heart and the world around you. Each decision to follow His leading—whether in extending kindness, offering a prayer, or standing for truth—becomes part of His unfolding plan. Reflect on how you can intentionally bring His light into the lives of others today. Through small but meaningful choices, His peace grows and His joy overflows into your relationships. Trust that your faithful actions will create lasting change, drawing others closer to the hope and renewal found in Him. Let your life reflect His grace and a testimony to His enduring presence.

NOTES:

EPILOGUE

Picture a river winding through a dry, barren land, carving pathways of life where none existed before. Its waters bring refreshment to thirsty soil, renewal to weary plants, and hope to places long abandoned. This is the power of prayer. As you conclude this devotional journey, reflect on the life-giving streams of prayer that have been shaping your heart, your home, and your world. The Lord's Prayer is not just a recitation; it is a river of living water, flowing from the throne of God and through every corner of your life.

Prayer is not merely words whispered into the silence. It is an invitation into divine partnership, a sacred act that transforms both the pray-er and the world. Like Corrie ten Boom, whose prayers sustained her through unimaginable trials, you've been invited into God's presence, to be refreshed and renewed. Each prayer you've prayed is a seed planted in faith, nurtured by His Spirit, and carried forward by your willingness to act. From your home to your neighborhood, to the ends of the earth, your prayers ripple outward, carrying His love in ways you may never see.

Let your home be the starting point of these ripples, where prayer forms the foundation of gratitude and forgiveness. In your neighborhood, let kindness—whether through a shared meal, a listening ear, or a simple smile—reflect the light of Christ. And in your community, step into challenges with the hands and feet of Jesus, serving and lifting others in His name. Every small act of obedience becomes a part of God's great redemption story.

The lessons of prayer do not end here; they are just beginning. As you prayed, "Your kingdom come, Your will be done," you aligned your heart with the purposes of heaven. Even when results are unseen, trust that your prayers, like rivers carving through rock, are shaping lives and circumstances in ways only God can orchestrate. Revelation 22:1-2 describes the ultimate fulfillment of this promise: "Then the angel showed me the river of the water of life, as clear as crystal, flowing from the throne of God and of the Lamb, down the middle of the great street of the city." Your prayers are part of this eternal current, a stream of God's justice, love, and renewal.

As you move forward, carry these truths with you. Prayer transforms. God provides. Love multiplies. Each ripple of prayer and love expands outward, becoming part of God's eternal plan to renew all things. May the words of the Shema and the Lord's Prayer remain your guide: love the Lord your God with all your heart, soul, mind, and strength, and love your neighbor as yourself.

Go forth with confidence. Let your prayers flow like streams of living water, refreshing the weary, renewing the broken, and spreading hope wherever they go. May the peace of Christ fill your heart and home, the Spirit embolden your steps, and the Father guide your journey. Every prayer, every act of love, becomes part of His kingdom's work, rippling through eternity and pointing others to the Source of all life. Amen.

THANK YOU

Thank you for purchasing *Living Waters: Unlock the Depths of the Lord's Prayer in 30 Days*. I know you had many options to choose from, and I'm deeply grateful that you chose this devotional. My prayer is that it has been a source of encouragement and inspiration, helping you draw closer to God and discover the joy of a deeper prayer life.

If this book has blessed you, I would be honored if you could take a few minutes to share your thoughts with an Amazon review.

Your feedback not only helps me grow as a writer but also serves as a testimony to others who may be searching for spiritual growth. Leaving a review on Amazon is a great first step in becoming a lightkeeper.

I also love hearing directly from my readers. If you'd like to share how this devotional has touched your life, your words will mean the world to me.

Thank you for supporting this mission to bring the hope, help, and healing of Jesus to the world.

SCRIPTURE VERSIONS

Scriptures marked (CEV) are from the Contemporary English Version® Copyright © 1995 by American Bible Society. Known for its clear, conversational tone, the CEV makes God's Word accessible to readers of all ages and literacy levels. All rights reserved.

Scriptures marked (ESV) are from The Holy Bible, English Standard Version® (ESV®) Copyright © 2001 by Crossway, a publishing ministry of Good News Publishers. Renowned for its balance of literary excellence and theological precision, the ESV remains a treasured resource for both personal study and public worship. All rights reserved.

Scriptures marked (HCSB) are from the Holman Christian Standard Bible® Copyright © 1999, 2000, 2002, 2003, 2009 by Holman Bible Publishers. Designed to convey the meaning of the original texts with clarity and precision, the HCSB brings timeless truth to contemporary readers.

Scriptures marked (NASB) are from the NEW AMERICAN STANDARD BIBLE®, Copyright © 1960, 1962, 1963, 1968, 1971, 1972, 1973, 1975, 1977, 1995 by The Lockman Foundation. Revered for its word-for-word accuracy, the NASB is a trusted choice for in-depth study and faithful interpretation of Scripture. Used by permission. All rights reserved.

Scriptures marked (NIV) are from THE HOLY BIBLE, NEW INTERNATIONAL VERSION®, NIV® Copyright © 1973, 1978, 1984, 2011 by Biblica, Inc.® Combining scholarly precision with readability, the NIV offers a

ABOUT THE AUTHOR

Dr. Daniel B. Lancaster (PhD, Church History and Missions) is an experienced leader in ministry, church planting, and global missions. Throughout his career, he has dedicated himself to equipping others to become passionate followers of Christ.

He planted two churches and trained over 5,000 people in Southeast Asia while serving as a strategy coordinator with the International Mission Board. He also served as Assistant Vice-President for University Ministries at Union University and currently serves as a global missionary at Cornerstone International.

In addition to his professional roles, Dr. Lancaster is the founder of *Every Home a Lighthouse*, a ministry dedicated to equipping homes around the world to shine as beacons of hope and healing through Jesus. *Every Home a Lighthouse* creates and distributes Christ-centered resources in multiple languages, focusing on the needs of the poor, persecuted, and forgotten.

Made in the USA
Monee, IL
17 February 2025

12247794R00115